T0318990

Cambridge Elements ≡

Elements in Critical Heritage Studies
edited by
Kristian Kristiansen, *University of Gothenburg*
Michael Rowlands, *UCL*
Francis Nyamnjoh, *University of Cape Town*
Astrid Swenson, *Bath University*
Shu-Li Wang, *Academia Sinica*
Ola Wetterberg, *University of Gothenburg*

PATRIMONIALITIES

Heritage vs. Property

Valdimar Tr. Hafstein
University of Iceland

Martin Skrydstrup
Copenhagen Business School

CAMBRIDGE
UNIVERSITY PRESS

University Printing House, Cambridge CB2 8BS, United Kingdom

One Liberty Plaza, 20th Floor, New York, NY 10006, USA

477 Williamstown Road, Port Melbourne, VIC 3207, Australia

314–321, 3rd Floor, Plot 3, Splendor Forum, Jasola District Centre, New Delhi – 110025, India

79 Anson Road, #06–04/06, Singapore 079906

Cambridge University Press is part of the University of Cambridge.

It furthers the University's mission by disseminating knowledge in the pursuit of education, learning, and research at the highest international levels of excellence.

www.cambridge.org
Information on this title: www.cambridge.org/9781108928380
DOI: 10.1017/9781108933629

© Valdimar Tr. Hafstein and Martin Skrydstrup 2020

First published 2020

A catalogue record for this publication is available from the British Library.

ISBN 978-1-108-92838-0 Paperback
ISSN 2632-7074 (online)
ISSN 2632-7066 (print)

Patrimonialities

Heritage vs. Property

Elements in Critical Heritage Studies

DOI: 10.1017/9781108933629
First published online: November 2020

Valdimar Tr. Hafstein
University of Iceland

Martin Skrydstrup
Copenhagen Business School

Author for correspondence: Valdimar Tr. Hafstein, vth@hi.is

Martin Skrydstrup, msk.msc@cbs.dk

Abstract: With empirical touchstones from Europe, North America, Africa, Asia, and the Pacific, the authors argue that heritage and property represent different approaches to subject formation, produce distinct bodies of expertise, and belong to different rationalities of government in a global patrimonial field: that cultural property is a technology of sovereignty, part of the order of the modern liberal state, but cultural heritage is a technology of reformation that cultivates responsible subjects and entangles them in networks of expertise and management. While particular case trajectories may shift back and forth from rights-based claims and resolutions under the sign of cultural property to ethical claims and solutions under the sign of cultural heritage, the authors contend that there is significant analytical purchase to be gained from their distinction. Using a critical, comparative approach, they make the case for a historically grounded and theoretically informed understanding of the difference between the two terms.

Keywords: cultural heritage, cultural property, sovereignty, reformation, repatriation

ISBNs: 9781108928380 (PB), 9781108933629 (OC)
ISSNs: 2632-7074 (online), ISSN 2632-7066 (print)

Contents

African cultural heritage can no longer remain a prisoner of European Museums.

Emmanuel Macron, 2018

Museums are democratising, inclusive and polyphonic spaces for critical dialogue about the pasts and the futures. Acknowledging and addressing the conflicts and challenges of the present, they hold artefacts and specimens in trust for society, safeguard diverse memories for future generations and guarantee equal rights and equal access to heritage for all people. Museums are . . . participatory and transparent, and work in active partnership with and for diverse communities to collect, preserve, research, interpret, exhibit, and enhance understandings of the world, aiming to contribute to human dignity and social justice, global equality and planetary wellbeing.

ICOM Executive Board, A New Definition of the Museum, 2019

I ask for Oluyenyetuye bronze of Ife
The moon says it is in Bonn

I ask for the Ogidigbonyingboyin mask of Benin
The moon says it is in London

I ask for Dinkowawa stool of Ashanti
The moon says it is in Paris

I ask for Togongorewa bust of Zimbabwe
The moon says it is in New York

I ask
I ask
I ask for the memory of Africa
The seasons say it is blowing in the wind

The hunchback cannot hide his burden

Niyi Osundare in *Horses of Memory* (1998)

1 The Patrimonial Field

Debates and Debacles

In November 2018, Felwine Sarr and Benedicte Savoy released a report commissioned by French President Emmanuel Macron, entitled *The Restitution of African Cultural Heritage: Toward a New Relational Ethics* (2018). In what has become a very influential document, Sarr and Savoy argue that the acquisition of cultural artifacts in Africa and their transfer to European metropoles was part of an orchestrated colonial enterprise resulting in cultural voids, the magnitude of which is poorly understood today (Sarr and Savoy, 2018, p. 15). Given this legacy, the report advocates seeing sub-Saharan Africa as a special case based on the dual premise that 95 percent of cultural artifacts from Africa are outside its borders and 60 percent of the continent's population is less than twenty years old. The implication, they argue, is memory loss, alienation, and cultural amnesia in contemporary Africa, specifically amongst the younger generation. The authors contend that this highlights the need for redistributive justice, historical reparations, memory work, and a new form of "relational ethics," where restitution has more relevance than ever before (Sarr and Savoy, 2018, p. 39).

The report is commissioned by the highest office in France, a nation that holds rich, extensive, and incomparable collections from sub-Saharan Africa. It also stands out in so far it is not a marginal voice, but draws on three high-level workshops with museum professionals, lawyers, and cultural bureaucrats, and on extensive consultation *within* the museum sector, the antiquities and art trade, and political spheres. The press has reported extensively on it (e.g. Jackson, 2018). The report defines concretely the chronological, juridical, museological, and financial frameworks for a major restitution program to Africa.

This new ambition of the French Presidency has sparked discussion and controversy beyond sub-Saharan Africa, but little concrete action as yet. As such, the report constitutes the latest contribution to five decades of the "who owns culture" debate, as the issue has repeatedly been pitched, since UNESCO adopted the 1970 Convention on the Means of Prohibiting and Preventing the Illicit Import, Export, and Transfer of Ownership of Cultural Property. We would argue that Macron's current initiative comes right out of and builds on the last two decades of this debate.

The current tone of this debate is framed by *The Declaration on the Importance and Value of Universal Museums* (*Declaration*, 2004) signed in 2003 by nineteen museums, all in Europe and North America. This

Declaration famously argued against return/restitution on the grounds that "universal museums" are custodians of encyclopedic collections, making them unique as repositories for all peoples, united under a single roof and accessible to the public at large. In this sense, the universal museum is like a central bank holding treasures in trust for humanity, providing universal access and knowledge for everyone endowed with curiosity. Going beyond the case-by-case approach and technicalities of legal frameworks and collection management policies, the *Declaration* emerged as a major counter-discourse to restitution claims.

Perhaps the most eloquent articulation of the *Declaration* was staged in May 2006 at a public symposium titled "Museums and the Collecting of Antiquities – Past, Present, and Future" at the New York Public Library. This significant event gathered the key signatories to the *Declaration* and their protagonists: The Director of the British Museum, Neil MacGregor; the Director of the Art Institute in Chicago, James Cuno; the Director of the Metropolitan Museum of Art, Philippe de Montebello; backed by Princeton

Figure 1 The New York Public Library (NYPL) in New York City, where the public symposium entitled "Museums and the Collecting of Antiquities – Past, Present and Future" took place on May 4, 2006. The event was organized and sponsored by the Association of Art Museum Directors (AAMD). The chosen venue resonated with the virtues and values of what the symposium called "the Encyclopedic or Cosmopolitan Museum as a legacy of the Enlightenment." Photograph by W & J (CC BY-SA 2.0).

philosopher Kwame Appiah and Stanford law Professor John Henry Merryman, united in New York City to give new currency to the term "cosmopolitanism" and breathe new life into the values of the Enlightenment.

The controversial Marion True case formed the subtext for this event, in which the curator of antiquities for the J. Paul Getty Museum in Los Angeles – one of the wealthiest museums in the world with one of the most respected curators – was indicted by the Italian government for taking part in the illicit trafficking of artifacts in 2005, ruining True's career and damaging the reputation of her institution. Not wanting to follow the Getty Museum down this road of disrepute, the Metropolitan Museum of Art announced in February 2006 that it would return a 2,500-year-old Greek vase known as the "Euphronios Krater" to Villa Giulia at the outskirts of Rome, within a larger partnership agreement. This announcement triggered a heated debate in 2006 about why New York City should lose an ancient Greek vase to a "sleepy" provincial museum in Italy. Three universal museum directors, backed by a philosopher and a lawyer, took a stand at the New York Public Library.

James Cuno defined the virtues of the kind of museums gathered at the New York Public Library:

> Encyclopedic museums, like the British Museum and the Metropolitan Museum of Art, with collections representative of the world's diverse artistic production, are a force for understanding, tolerance, and the dissipation of ignorance, superstition and prejudice about the world. They are a legacy of the Enlightenment and are dedicated to the principle that access to the full diversity of human artistic industry promotes the polymeric ideal of discovering and understanding the whole of human knowledge and improve and advance the condition of our species in the world we inhabit. (May 4, 2006; recording on file with the authors)

Cuno maintained that the emergence of cultural property laws and UNESCO conventions in the second half of the twentieth century was an "invention of nationalism," which "discouraged the building of encyclopedic collections. This comes at a time when the world is increasingly divided along ideological, political, and cultural lines, and thus challenges the very principles on which the Encyclopedic Museum as an enlightenment museum was founded" (May 4, 2006; recording on file with the authors).

Princeton philosopher, Kwame Anthony Appiah, picked up where Cuno left off and juxtaposed cosmopolitanism and nationalism, which "stood side by side in a close relationship for a long time. What has happened is that the balance between nationalism and cosmopolitanism has gone completely to the wrong side," Appiah deplored, and paused before adding: "the right side being the centre." "Now," he denounced, "we have a system which looks like its point is to stop the movement of culture across national borders":

> It looks like the UNESCO regulations seem to have behind them the thought that every object is the expression of some national *Geist* – this is a Herderian idea – and that this Geist should live at home. But that's to forget the cosmopolitan side, which says that every object is indeed an expression of a *Geist*, but human beings need to share the products of their communities across borders. We need to understand each other's cultures, in part because that is the way which we can understand our identity as human beings. (May 4, 2006; recording on file with the authors)

From this creative tension between nationalism and cosmopolitanism, Appiah developed the argument that UNESCO regulations are antithetical to the cosmopolitan ideal, suggesting that if the proliferation of nationalist regulations continued unabated then one thing was certain: "There will be no more encyclopedic museums":

> In particular, there will be no encyclopedic museums in Africa. That would be a tragedy, in my opinion. There was once an encyclopedic museum in Kumasi, where I grew up. It was destroyed by the British and the objects were looted. I am not an enthusiast for looting, but if we wanted to try to do again what the Ashanti King did, one of the main obstacles to our doing so would be a bunch of UNESCO regulations. This is the irony, since the King of Ashanti who started that museum did so because he was inspired by the story of the British Museum. (May 4, 2006; recording on file with the authors)

For the arguments that art knows no national borders; that art should travel without regulation; and that the encyclopedic project was not imperialism with a white face, but an idea that once caught on in Kumasi, Appiah received long and standing applause in the New York Public Library.

Neil MacGregor picked up Cuno's lead and used the French Enlightenment project to define the kind of context that his institution could provide for objects:

> In the introduction to the seventh volume of the *Encyclopédie* in the mid-1760s, Diderot talks about the endeavor to gather universal knowledge, so that we can bring our fellow men to love each other, tolerate each other and to recognize the superiority of universal morality over the particular one. That's what the context of the universal museum was meant to do. May 4, 2006; recording on file with the authors)

Having evoked this kind of context – one that differed radically from the particular historical-cultural context prevalent in Sarr and Savoy's 2018 report – MacGregor showed a number of concrete objects exhibited in the British

Museum, each one of which had scattered prejudices and stereotypes about the world in the sense of Diderot's notion of universal knowledge: from the Oldowai Gorge axes excavated in Tanzania by physical anthropologist Richard Leakey, discovered in the late 1920s, which put the beginnings of civilization firmly in Africa, thus subverting hierarchies at the time, to a stool acquired in 2002 built by weapons, showing that Mozambique could not have had a civil war without the rest of the world but also that Africa had found a way to decommission weapons, which Belfast had not, reversing usual assumptions about who has to learn from whom. According to MacGregor, the unique collections of universal museums enabled this universal knowledge production, and that justified removing objects (be that the Benin Bronzes or the fossil record of humanity) from their original contexts to encyclopedic museums. And the objects remaining there.

Less than a year after this powerful articulation of the neo-Enlightenment position by its most eloquent protagonists in New York City, UNESCO headquarters in Paris responded with a public debate entitled *Universality and Cultural Memory: New Challenges for Museums.* This latter debate serves as subtext to the Sarr and Savoy 2018 report, as these attempts to realign universality and cultural memory reverberate throughout their report. Prof.

Figure 2 UNESCO Headquarters at Place Fontenoy, Paris. Photograph by Matthias Ripp (CC BY-SA).

Krzysztof Pomian, an art historian, opened the debate and coined the key question, "To whom does a heritage belong? To humankind or to a given people?" Pomian argued that works of art are produced by individuals, not by peoples and that "works of art embody the dignity and become visible emblems of the identity of a particular group, but other groups can be touched or moved by such works of art as well" (February 5, 2007; recording on file with the authors). This conception of material artifacts as collectively vested with identities, should make Pomian positive toward restitution, but he had one overriding reservation: "Top priority should be given to conservation. There is no reason to return an object if it is in danger of damage" (February 5, 2007; recording on file with the authors).

Another key player in the debate who directly challenged the notion of "cosmo-politanism" set out in New York was the Chair of ICOM's Ethics Committee, Bernice Murphy: "Last year in New York, Philippe de Montebello defined his idea of the universal museum as 'the cultural family tree where all people can find their roots'" (February 5, 2007; recording on file with the authors). Murphy took issue with this "high-minded idea of the universal museum" by venturing to Melbourne arguing that Montebello's Museum in Manhattan:

> showed only the memory patterns of one culture at work – the collecting culture. The cultural family tree in New York, demonstrates the loss and erasure of the memory structures of the cultures collected. Therefore, for me, Philippe de Montebello's image of the universal museum as the cultural family tree where all people can find their roots cannot possibly express what is happening. (February 5, 2007; recording on file with the authors)

According to Murphy, what was happening to the objects collected among Aboriginals was this:

> All of these spears and shields and other things that were shown in the New York exhibition have come from different peoples of different kinship, different traditions, different languages, and the original producers would have been horrified to find their cultural items mixed up with foreign items in this way, destroying all meanings that are important to the producing cultures, or what is here being called the "source cultures." The producing cultures – many of them continuing and flourishing today – give meaning to any particular item only through the total ensemble of living relationships and practices that emanate from one particular people, language and tradition. (February 5, 2007; recording on file with the authors)

Going beyond the politics of museum display, Murphy took issue with the very notion of "universality." She argued that the challenge to encyclopedic museums did not come from afar in the shape of restitution claims; rather, it came from within:

Encyclopedic museums now face intense pressures as we know but, I want to emphasize, that pressure comes not from somewhere else far away. The pressures are coming from within the history of the discourse of universality itself, which has given birth to a legacy of ideas such as the dignity of humankind, fundamental human rights, ideas of distributive justice, liberty for all and the right of diverse societies to their own cultural practices and self-determination. All these tensions come from within the heritage of the universal discourse. (February 5, 2007; recording on file with the authors)

Murphy argued, in other words, that the Enlightenment the "cosmopolitans" claimed as their own was in fact an emancipatory source of universal justice and equal rights, which the "cosmopolitans" conveniently ignored, confining themselves to a form of conservatism that foreclosed other ontologies; their universalism, she suggested, verged on a provincial orthodoxy.

The same decade as the *Declaration on the Value of Universal Museums* was crafted, we saw the inauguration of two prestigious institutions built as antipodes to the *Declaration*. First, in September 2004, the *National Museum*

Figure 3 The National Museum of the American Indian, located on the National Mall in Washington, DC, with a clear view of Capitol Hill. The NMAI opened on September 21, 2004, to the largest assembly of Indigenous Peoples in Washington, DC, to this time. Its architectural features draw on a multitude of Native American design cosmologies. Photograph by O Palsson (CC BY 2.0).

Figure 4 Entry to the new Acropolis Museum in Athens, where the conference "Return of Cultural Objects to their Countries of Origin" took place in March 2008, just before the official inauguration of the Museum itself. This conference was organized and sponsored by the Greek Ministry of Culture. Photograph by Martin Skrydstrup.

of the American Indian opened in Washington, DC, recognizing "America's First Citizens" on the National Mall and providing a new home for artifacts and ancestral remains repatriated with recourse to NAGPRA (Native American Graves Protection and Repatriation Act, 1990). Second, in March 2008, the *New Acropolis Museum* opened in Athens, an architectural counter-argument to the *Declaration*, with the proclaimed purpose to bring back the Parthenon sculptures, held by the British Museum, to the "blue skies of Attica."

We hope we have brought into view the tug-of-war between forces of pull and push, or centripetal and centrifugal gravity, which are at work in the discursive fields and institutional spaces of what we call the global patrimonial field. Common to all these debates, right up to French President Macron's current initiative and the Sarr and Savoy report, is that they hardly distinguish between cultural heritage and cultural property. We argue that the debates and debacles we have rendered here can be illuminated and even rethought by careful conceptual labor, departing from a historical distinction between the two concepts and linking them to distinct governmentalities.

Sovereignty and Reformation:
Cultural Property vs. Cultural Heritage

A persisting problem for the critical study of cultural property is how to conceptualize differences in the ways in which national and indigenous claims are shaped and legitimated. The coupling of identity and indigeneity with ownership and rights mobilized in claims have been read analytically as identity politics (Handler, 1988), nation building (Li, 2001), resistance (Miller, 1995), postcolonial mimesis (Bhabha, 1994), alternative modernities (Coombe, 2003), forms of ethno-commodification (Comaroff and Comaroff, 2009), and as a "provincializing move that destabilizes our certainty about what is local and what is global" (Geismar, 2013). It seems to us that such readings hinge on how we configure "case studies" vis-à-vis larger processes of state formations.

In what follows, we cut a different pathway through these conundrums. We present a sustained argument, which reframes the debate about how to read claims. Our argument is based on contrasts between cultural property and cultural heritage and between distinct technologies of governmentality, which we argue are associated with these terms. Thus, specific technologies of governmentality produce distinct sets of claims. The stepping stones in our argument are the following: first, we set out the nominal distinctions between property and heritage, then we show how *property* is associated with technologies of *sovereignty*, and *heritage* with technologies of *reformation*, and finally we discuss how these technologies of governmentality can coexist in single-case trajectories.

In an article published in the first volume of the *International Journal of Cultural Property* in 1992, Lyndel V. Prott and Patrick J. O. Keefe contrast the terms "cultural property" and "cultural heritage." Whereas cultural property denotes ownership and exclusivity, they contend, cultural heritage denotes a relationship of responsibility, custodianship, and sharing. The thrust of their argument is that the time had come for the latter concept to succeed and supplant the former: "Is it time for law and lawyers to recognize that the term 'cultural heritage' is rightfully superseding that of 'cultural property'? To our minds the answer can only be 'Yes'" (Prott and O'Keefe, 1992). In conclusion, they add:

> The concept of the "cultural heritage" is one well recognized and universally used by historians, archaeologists, anthropologists and other researchers of human life both past and present. They virtually never use the term "property" unless in a legal context. In the law which has embodied the notion of "property" it is now coming to be recognized that this is inadequate and inappropriate for the range of matters covered by the concept of the "cultural heritage." (p. 319)

Eight years later, Janet Blake, legal scholar and long-term UNESCO consultant, suggests that although the "relationship between 'cultural property' and 'cultural heritage' is unclear, appearing interchangeable in some cases, . . . 'cultural heritage' has now become the term of art in international law since it is capable of encompassing [a] much broader range of possible elements" (Blake, 2000, p. 67). In a book on *International Cultural Heritage Law* from 2015, Blake reaffirms that "cultural property" is "far too limited a term" and therefore now "much less widely used and the alternative cultural heritage is generally favoured" (Blake, 2015, p. 8).

On the other hand, Manlio Frigo, another legal scholar, observes that "the concepts of cultural heritage and cultural property practically never appear simultaneously as complementary notions in the same legal text" (Frigo, 2004, p. 376), which may be taken to indicate that in fact they have distinct functions and relate to legal regimes that are at least partly separate. Frigo suggests that this relationship is further complicated by different national terminologies (p. 370), a claim which legal anthropologist Rosemary Coombe dismisses, along with any attempts to distinguish between the two concepts:

> Such interpretive difficulties now seem provincial. In any case, these promise only to proliferate as these categories expand, their distinction implodes, and their subject matter and fields of reference proliferate. (Coombe, 2009, p. 394)

We take issue with Coombe's position as well as with the claims by Prott and O'Keefe and by Blake that the concept of heritage has superseded or ought to take the place of cultural property. As we understand them, these concepts operate within a global patrimonial field with a proliferating variety of actors: states, intergovernmental organizations, transnational NGOs, indigenous peoples, local communities, museums, archives, institutions, universities, scholars, and experts. The patrimonial field is governed by national and international regimes, some of which gravitate toward a rights-based approach to protection and dispute management under the sign of cultural property, while others gravitate toward an ethical approach to conservation and safeguarding under the sign of cultural heritage. Rights-based regimes of cultural property come with their own set of national laws and international conventions, committees, discourses, and forms of expertise and while there are certainly overlaps, these can be distinguished from corresponding institutions of the ethical regimes of cultural heritage operating in the same global patrimonial field. We argue that the two correspond to distinct governmental rationalities and modes of subject formation: that cultural property is a technology of sovereignty and cultural heritage a technology of reformation.

Outline of the Argument

In the following sections, we elaborate this thesis through a series of examples or case studies from Europe, North America, Africa, Asia, and the Pacific, exploring its heuristic value (i.e. the insights it affords into patrimonial discourses and practices) and adding greater nuance to the distinction through empirical resistance and ethnographic surprise. Section 2 explores cultural property as a technology of sovereignty. From the Hague Convention to NAGPRA, we argue that claims for the restitution or return of cultural property assert sovereign powers and affirm integrity in the face of foreign rule, foreign science, and globalized markets; cultural property claims thus play a part in shaping sovereign subjects, with more or less success.

After discussing the concept of sovereignty, the section analyzes first the political uses of the Lewis Chessmen in the debate over Scotland's future within or without the United Kingdom. Next, it turns to Greek claims for the restitution of the Parthenon sculptures, the British Museum's reframing of the sculptures as part of a universal museum for humankind, and the Greek government's subsequent counter-framing of its claim in terms of universal heritage and the global debt to Greece. Running parallel to the case of the Parthenon sculptures is a third one involving a Kwakwaka'wakw ceremonial mask held by the British Museum; forging an alliance between a nation-state and a First Nation against the universal museum. Together these three cases illustrate claim-making as a technology of sovereignty at different scales. Finally, Section 2 closes with a consideration of NAGPRA as a machine for producing sovereignty at the subnational level through a case study of the return of a wooden figure (*ki'ila'au*) to Hawaii from the Museum of Natural History and Planetarium in Providence.

In contrast, Section 3 considers cultural heritage as a technology of reformation. While the regime of cultural property defines rights, the heritage regime defines responsibilities; the former is rights-based, the latter ethical. Although claims staked within both regimes help to constitute collective subjects, the subject of cultural property tends to be exclusive, subject to misappropriation and entitled to restitution; the subject of cultural heritage tends rather to be inclusive, a collective "we" that should stand together to prevent degradation and loss. The regime of cultural heritage has taken shape in the past half century as one part of a wider turn to participation across the policy spectrum, engaging communities through participatory techniques in a project of *Bildung* or self-cultivation, fostering new forms of subjectivity and cultivating the capacity for action. As a technology of reformation, we argue that safeguarding is best understood as a part of the arts of governing, a process that teaches people to have a heritage, to value it, to identify with it, and to preserve it, aligning their ambitions and practices with policies from the centers of calculation through an infusion of expertise, training, and cooperation.

Case studies from Malawi, India, and Morocco demonstrate the analytical affordance of this understanding of cultural heritage and flesh out the argument with empirical detail. The first one relates what happens when a popular medical practice, Vimbuza, is reframed as intangible cultural heritage and actively safeguarded, recalibrating the relationship of practitioners, patients, and critics to the practice and reinterpreting it through modes of display characteristic of heritage (such as the festival). The manner in which cultural heritage reforms the relationships that people have with their environment and practices is also brought out in the story of the elevation of Kutiyattam Sanskrit Theater to the status of the intangible heritage of humanity, the new institutions built in response to its heritagization and the reactions of Kutiyattam artists to their own newfound status elevation and to the structures that govern their work. Finally, the story of how the Jemaa el Fna marketplace in Marrakech was saved from the tooth of the bulldozer through its heritagization brings out the contradictions of cultural heritage as a technology of reformation, which saves its object only by transforming it.

Section 4 adds nuance and a further twist to our argument, historicizing the contrast between cultural property and cultural heritage. In this section on different patrimonialities, we consider three distinct cases in which a claim staked under the sign of sovereignty for the restitution of cultural property to its rightful owners has been answered with offers of sharing, loans, and common responsibility for common cultural heritage backed up by an infusion of expertise and permanent mechanisms for engagement. Thus, having severed longstanding political ties with its former rulers in Denmark, a newly sovereign Iceland asked the Danish government to return the manuscripts of its medieval literature held in archives and centers of learning in Copenhagen; instead, Icelanders were offered a partnership, sharing the manuscripts of which two different halves would be housed in sister institutes in each country. This model of partition and partnership was replicated in the so-called UTIMUT case, when the National Museum of Denmark transferred part of its ethnographic and archeological holdings from Copenhagen to the National Museum of Greenland according to curatorial criteria worked out between these institutions, which involved the creation of a new museum building and facilities as part of the capacity building involved in this sharing of heritage. Finally, the loan of a ceremonial mask held by the British Museum to the Kwakwaka'wakw First Nation shows how a claim of exclusive ownership is deflected through curatorial cunning and turned into a mechanism for engagement; the mask moves from under the sign of cultural property to under the sign of cultural heritage and is subject at once to technologies of sovereignty and reformation.

Finally, Section 5 sums up our argument for an historically grounded and theoretically informed understanding of the distinction between cultural property and cultural heritage. It demonstrates, moreover, how particular case trajectories may shift back and forth from rights-based claims and resolutions under the sign of cultural property to ethical claims and solutions under the sign of cultural heritage, returning once more to a couple of the cases explored in the following chapters: renewed claims by Iceland's government for the return of the medieval manuscripts that still remain in Denmark and the relaunching of claims to the Parthenon Sculptures on the occasion of the 200th birthday of the Greek nation. We close by considering the various claims to unity, integrity, and wholeness in the case trajectories and asking what insight these concepts afford into different patrimonialities.

2 Cultural Property as a Technology of Sovereignty

When Lyndel V. Prott and Patrick Keefe set out the contrast between cultural property and cultural heritage, Prott had recently been appointed Chief of the International Standards Section in the Division of Cultural Heritage of the United Nations Educational, Scientific, and Cultural Organization (UNESCO), where she was in charge of conventions for cultural property and cultural heritage. Since its founding in 1946, UNESCO has developed a series of such legal instruments, beginning in 1954 with the Convention for the Protection of Cultural Property in the Event of Armed Conflict, often referred to as the Hague Convention for short. "Recognizing that cultural property has suffered grave damage during recent armed conflicts," the Hague Convention begins, and "Being convinced that damage to *cultural property belonging to any people whatsoever* means damage to the *cultural heritage of all mankind*" (our emphasis), the states parties to the convention agree to take on various obligations to protect cultural property from theft and destruction. As is evident from the preamble, cultural property and cultural heritage both emerged in international law through the Hague Convention, already recognizably distinct: in the quoted sentences, cultural property belongs to a people, whereas cultural heritage is attributed to mankind. Cultural heritage and cultural property were thus coined as international legal concepts within a decade of the end of the WWII and as part of a new world order represented by the United Nations.

Since its inception, UNESCO has been the engine driving the development of regimes of cultural property and cultural heritage. Up until the 1970s, its efforts focused on the legal protection of cultural property. Following up on the Hague

Convention, in 1970, UNESCO's member states adopted the Convention on the Means of Prohibiting and Preventing the Illicit Import, Export and Transfer of Ownership of Cultural Property (based on UNESCO's Recommendation of the same name from 1964) and, in 1978, founded an Intergovernmental Committee for Promoting the Return of Cultural Property to its Countries of Origin or its Restitution in case of Illicit Appropriation. As the titles of the 1970 convention and the committee make clear, cultural property is, at its inception, a national concept, used in the context of claims for the return or restitution of historical artifacts from one state to another. UNESCO's instruments, binding for states that ratify them, lend to such claims the force of international law.

At the national level, some regimes of cultural property also provide legal grounds for peoples, tribes, or communities within national borders to stake claims on state institutions for the repatriation of artifacts from their collections to their original holders. In the patrimonial field, the very term "repatriation" was first inscribed into law by the passage of the National Museum of the American Indian Act (NMAIA) in 1989, followed by the Native American Graves Protection and Repatriation Act (NAGPRA) one year later. The term repatriation – literally meaning back to the father's land – has since then diffused into a general designation for acts of return, albeit its legal use is restricted to the national domains of settler-colonies. Historically, NMAIA and NAGPRA may represent the apex of the idea of cultural property as the exclusive property of lineal descendants or tribes (*patria*) through a technology that produces and asserts the sovereignty of its claimants.

The claims that regimes of cultural property recognize and validate are claims to objects which colonialism, capitalism, and science have transported in their common luggage. These claims propose now to reverse their trajectories and return the objects to their countries of origin or to their rightful owners within settler colonial societies. Claims to cultural property are usually staked in the aftermath of violence: of war or colonial rule, or both. The claims assert sovereign powers and they affirm cultural integrity in the face of foreign invasion and foreign rule, globalized markets, and foreign science. Cultural property claims thus help form sovereign subjects, whether independent peoples or semiautonomous social collectives such as communities and tribes. In other words, claims to cultural property are a technology of sovereignty.

Sovereignty is typically understood as a property of nation-states, often taken to mean that a state is sovereign when it governs its own *dominium* independently; what Hannah Arendt characterized as "uncompromising self-sufficiency and mastership" (Arendt, 1958, p. 234). The various congruencies between notions of liberal individualism and this modernist notion of sovereign state agency became – not surprisingly – the target for postmodern critiques of various bents. Perhaps most famously, Giorgio Agamben argued that sovereignty is in fact indistinguishable from a permanent state of exception (Agamben, 1998), drawing on Carl Schmitt's idea of sovereignty as the exception to rules (Schmitt, 2005 [1922]). Less well known is Jacques Derrida's intervention, which argued that "sovereignty" designates "unconditional expenditure" (Derrida, 1978), drawing on George Bataille's notion that sovereign action is a form of agency undertaken without any expectations of reciprocity/compensation. Michael Brown's critique of the "talismanic properties" of the principle of sovereignty (Brown, 2003, p. 224), which he finds antithetical to "complex cultural flows" (p. 225) and which according to him "has led proponents of Total Heritage Protection to focus on customary law as the solution for conflicts over intellectual property" (p. 225), clearly leans on the modernist notion of sovereignty that Arendt described.

Our concept of "technologies of sovereignty" builds in part on Haidy Geismar's argument that "property is an implementation of sovereignty everywhere, whether or not it is acknowledged as such" (Geismar, 2013, p. 18). However, where Geismar aims to capture indigenous aspirations to sovereignty – where property is the necessary medium and recognition sets the terms for acknowledgment – our analytical prism anchors sovereignty in *technologies of governmentality*. By this we mean sovereignty *through* the technology of recognition, infused by expertise.

The Lewis Chessmen

A telling example of how claims to cultural property are enlisted in the formation of sovereign subjects may be gleaned from a speech by Alex Salmond, Scotland's First Minister, in 2007, in which he deplores the fact, "utterly unacceptable" in his view, that the Lewis Chessmen (a medieval collection of ninety-three chess pieces) are still "scattered around Britain." "And you can be assured," Salmond declares, "that I will continue campaigning for a united set of Lewis Chessmen in an independent Scotland" (Salmond, 2007). Salmond's demand for the return of cultural property is inseparable from his claim to national sovereignty; as we argue here, the former is a technology to produce the latter.

Salmond's claim is also telling, however, of the complex field within which cultural property is enlisted as a technology of sovereignty. What is commonly referred to as the Lewis Chessmen is a hoard of gaming pieces found in Uig, Isle of Lewis, in the Outer Hebrides (aka the Western Isles) in 1831. Carved from walrus ivory and whale's teeth, with elaborate representations of seated kings

and queens, mounted knights, bishops in miters, warders, and pawns, the pieces
found their way into the antiquities market in Edinburgh that same year when
Roderick Ririe from Lewis sold them to two separate buyers. A noted Scottish
collector, Charles Kirkpatrick Sharpe, bought ten of these gaming pieces while
J. A. Forrest, a local dealer, bought the remaining eighty-two. Later that
same year, Forrest sold his eighty-two pieces to the British Museum (see
Figure 5). Sharpe acquired one more chess piece from another source and
upon his death in 1851, his eleven chessmen were sold to Lord
Londesborough; they came to the Scotland's National Museum upon the sale
of Londesborough's collection in 1888 (Caldwell et al., 2009, pp. 168–172).

The consensus among archeologists and art historians is that the pieces were
most likely made by craftsmen in Norway in the twelfth or thirteenth centuries.
In this period, the Outer Hebrides were under Norse control; they were ruled by
the kings of Norway from 1098 until they were yielded to the Kingdom of
Scotland in 1266. No one knows exactly how the chess pieces found their way to
the Isle of Lewis, but various stories account for their travels. The websites of
the British Museum and National Museums Scotland provide conflicting
accounts in support of diverging claims on the chess pieces. The British

Figure 5 Nine Lewis Chessmen at the British Museum. © Trustees of the
British Museum.

Museum thus tells its visitors that "the Lewis Chessmen are an important symbol of European civilisation":

> These chess pieces form a remarkable group of iconic objects within the world collection of the British Museum. They were probably made in Trondheim, Norway, about AD 1150–1200. At this period, the Western Isles, where the chess pieces were found, were part of the Kingdom of Norway, not Scotland. It seems likely they were buried for safe keeping on route to be traded in Ireland. . . . It is possible that they originally belonged to a merchant travelling from Norway to Ireland. (British Museum Press Release, 2018)

Going well beyond mere description, the entire narrative supports the placement of the gaming pieces in the British Museum, which "exists to tell the story of cultural achievement throughout the world" and "allows the public to re-examine cultural identities and explore the complex network of interconnected world cultures." The only mention of Scotland is preceded by negation: "not." The story ("likely" and "possible") of the traveling merchant, who buried his wares in Lewis and did not survive to recover them, is the only explanation given for the presence of the gaming pieces in the Hebrides ("not Scotland"). By this account, it is merely an accident that the chessmen were lost and found in Lewis.

But this story of origins is not the only one in circulation and no consensus surrounds it (unlike the Scandinavian origin of the pieces). In fact, archeologists at National Museums Scotland who worked for years on the chess pieces in preparation for a major touring exhibition, "Lewis Chessmen: Unmasked" (produced jointly with the British Museum in 2010), maintain that "a lost merchant's stock-in-trade is but one, and probably the least plausible, of possibilities for the hoard being found in Lewis" (Caldwell et al., 2009, p. 167). Rather, they see no impediments to "placing its use in Lewis as the prized possession of a local prince, nobleman or senior churchman" (p. 197). "The most obvious explanation," they maintain, is "that it belonged in Lewis to a person, and in a society, which valued its contents as gaming pieces. Indeed, it is significant that, within Britain, the only other ivory chessmen of similar quality to those from Lewis also have West Highland provenances" – and may now be found in the collection of National Museums Scotland (p. 168).

On the website of National Museums Scotland, one of these archeologists, Mark A. Hall, describes his lifelong fascination with the Lewis Chessmen:

> No matter how briefly gazed upon, they transport me immediately across time and space to a somewhat draughty and warmly-lit hall on Lewis, where they accumulated in part at least as gifts and perhaps in part as booty, and where they were used as the earnest playthings of adults, the less serious playthings of children and as talismanic watchers of the room(s) they furnished. (Hall, 2010)

Unpacking these conflicting narratives, it is clear that whereas one lends itself to Salmond's demand for the return of cultural property from England to "an independent Scotland," the other is crafted to counter that claim. Indeed, the British Museum tells us that it "has made the Lewis Chessmen in its collection freely accessible since their acquisition in the nineteenth century" and "they are hugely popular with the Museum's visitors who can admire them alongside other masterpieces of European civilisation and can compare and contrast them to other world cultures" (British Museum Press Release, 2018).

Alex Salmond's assurance in 2007 that he would "continue campaigning for a united set of Lewis Chessmen in an independent Scotland" reaffirmed the claim he staked already in 1996, when he argued in an interview with the *Sunday Times* that "just as the Elgin marbles should be restored to Greece . . . so should ancient artefacts come home to Scotland. There is no justification for them to remain in England" (Robertson, 1996).

In the Scottish Parliament, Liberal Democratic MP Hugh O'Donnell asked the Scottish Culture Minister, Linda Fabiani, whether the Scottish government's position on the Lewis Chessmen reflects "the Scottish Government's general policy on repatriating artefacts? Does the minister have a list of items that are held in Scottish collections that she proposes to return to their original homes?" And, moreover, "Does she support the return of the Elgin marbles to the people of Greece?" Fabiani responded that every case ought to be considered on its own merits, but she hastened to add, "The case for the Lewis Chessmen is particularly strong, and there is no reason whatsoever why, under the current United Kingdom settlement, the British Museum should not return the chessmen to the National Museum of Scotland." "Of course," she prodded, alluding to the underlying rationale of cultural property as a technology of sovereignty, "come independence, how such things are dealt with will change" (*Scottish Parliamentary Business Report*, 2008, pp. 11007–11008).

Other members of Salmond's Scottish National Party have upheld the claim over the years. When the British Museum and the BBC advertised a radio series on the "History of the World in 100 Objects" in 2010 with posters in underground stations depicting some of these objects, Angus MacNeil, an MP representing the Western Isles, was incensed. On February 22, MacNeil tabled a motion in the British House of Commons, signed by sixteen MPs from across the political spectrum:

> That this House deplores the historical airbrushing of the Lewis Chessmen by the British Museum in a poster campaign advertising the Museum which shows a picture of a Lewis Chessman with a date caption AD 1150–1200 and the word Norway below; further deplores the fact that references to Lewis or the Hebrides are nowhere to be seen; and notes that the only thing certain

about the chessmen, from the expansive European Norse society, is that they are made from walrus ivory or whale teeth and that they were found on the Isle of Lewis in 1831. (UK Parliament Early Day Motions, 2010, EDM #892).

In a speech in parliament on March 10, MacNeil called for the return of the chessmen to Lewis. He argued:

> Surely it is best, if historical artefacts are retained in the area where they are found. Whether by Act of Parliament or an alteration in museum policy, something must change because what made sense in the 19th century may now be a dated approach. Why must everything be in London? It seems to be historical centralisation and imperialism. . . . Why the British Museum has a colonial attitude of keeping artefacts that belong to another place and another people is beyond me. (UK Parliament Westminster Hall 2010, vol. 507, col. 124WH-125WH)

Margaret Hodge, UK Culture Minister, responded with a spirited defense for the principle of universal museums as "worldwide centres of learning and interpretation" and as "part of a wider international web of information sharing." Addressing Angus MacNeil directly, Hodge added:

> As the hon. Gentleman knows, I profoundly disagree with the underlying premise of his argument that culture is to be enjoyed only by the nation most closely identified with it. . . . [I]f beautiful artefacts are created, they should be enjoyed as widely as possible, not just in one nation. They do not enhance the lives of just one community, but of all of us in all our communities. The advent of digitisation enables us to share more widely the wonderful treasures that we are privileged to enjoy in our great national museums.

Bob Spink, a representative of the UK Independence Party from Essex, called the minister on her digitisation argument, which he suggested actually "works in both directions": "If the British Museum, for instance, were to move a third of the artefacts back to Lewis, digitisation would mean that there was no impediment to the scholarship of the museum and would increase world knowledge and access to those wonderful objects" (UK Parliament Westminster Hall 2010, vol. 507, col. 128WH-129WH).

Drawing a parallel to an earlier repatriation case in Scotland, Angus MacNeil made reference to the Ghost Shirt of a Sioux warrior killed at Wounded Knee in 1890. A member of Buffalo Bill's Wild West Traveling Show sold the bloodstained and bulletpierced shirt, along with other Native American objects, to the Kelvingrove Museum in Glasgow in 1891, and it was on display at the museum until 1999. Following a four-year campaign for the shirt's return by the Wounded Knee Association, the Glasgow City Council voted to return the shirt to the Lakota people, overturning an earlier decision by the Director of

Glasgow Museums to retain the shirt (Select Committee on Culture, Media and Sport, 2000).

"I am impressed," Angus MacNeil told his peers in parliament, "that the Kelvingrove museum in Glasgow returned a ghost dance shirt belonging to the Oglala Sioux after their repeated attempts to have it repatriated" (UK Parliament Westminster Hall 2010, vol. 507, col. 125WH). His colleague from the Scottish National Party, John Mason, agreed: "We felt that the shirt that was mentioned earlier should go back to North America, as that is where it would be better placed, and I give respect to Glasgow city council for that" (UK Parliament Westminster Hall 2010, vol. 507, col. 129WH).

The minister, Margaret Hodge, respectfully disagreed with the logic underlying this parallel, and suggested a more modest alternative to repatriation and return: loans and cooperation.

> However, things are where they are, and if we wish them to be shared, the British Museum has an excellent, first-class record in both collaboration and giving out loans. . . . There are ways of sharing that do not necessarily reside in ownership. I think that the British Museum excels in its record of trying to ensure that it shares its wonders with as wide an audience as possible. (UK Parliament Westminster Hall 2010, vol. 507, col. 129WH)

Indeed, the practice of lending is key to the British Museum's presentation of the Lewis Chessmen online. It is significant in our context that as part of its presentation, the museum highlights the fact that it lent the chessmen for exhibitions in Edinburgh, Aberdeen, Shetland, and Stornoway (but glides without a whisper past their recent loans to Shanghai, Beijing, Brisbane, Perth, Kobe, Tokyo, Paris, New York, Berlin, Barcelona, Madrid, Trondheim, Rome, Copenhagen, etc.). This bolsters a corollary argument: as a universal museum "of the world for the world," the British Museum "is committed to maintaining and extending access to the Lewis Chessmen for its audiences across the UK and the world." In particular, the museum's presentation of the chess pieces emphasizes its commitment to interested audiences in the Hebrides and elsewhere in Scotland, obviating (one deduces) the need for their formal return.

Hodge responded to Salmond's call for the return of the chessmen in an article published in *The Scotsman* in January 2008. Raising the specter of returning to Egypt "the glorious mummies and antiquities" in the National Museum in Edinburgh and repatriating the "the Burrell's Impressionist paintings" to France, she dismisses the claim: "It's a lot of nonsense, isn't it?" Invoking once more the magic bullet of collection loans and expert cooperation, Hodge continues: "Mr Salmond's clarion call is all about creating conflict, not culture. It's an ounce of policy mixed with a pound of posturing, because museums and galleries in the 21st century do not have static collections. They lend and borrow. They acquire." Reciting the repeated travels of the chessmen to museums in Scotland, England, and the United States, she notes that they "work for their keep" and concludes, "I believe that amicable arrangements between institutions are fine examples of what a living cultural policy should look like" (Hodge, 2008).

This counter-presentation of the Lewis Chessmen not as exclusive cultural property (subject to return) but as inclusive cultural heritage (held by the British Museum for the world) is now completed by the "long-term loan" of six of these gaming pieces; not to National Museums Scotland, mind you, but back to Lewis. As part of a loan agreement between Comhairle nan Eilean Siar (the Western Isles Council) and the British Museum, the six chessmen are the main attraction of the Museum nan Eilean, which opened in a purpose-built extension to Lews Castle in Stornoway in 2016. Bypassing Edinburgh, the long-term loan of the chessmen to Lewis as the central attraction of a museum built to house them secures and showcases strong lines of communication between London and Lewis, expert cooperation between the universal museum and the local museum without stopping at the national museum. Further "scattering" the hoard of gaming pieces, the long-term loan and the partnership undermine the campaign for "a united set of Lewis Chessmen in an independent Scotland." Responding to claims of cultural property from Scotland, the British Museum thus frames the Lewis Chessmen as cultural heritage.

The Parthenon Sculptures

The case of the Parthenon sculptures lends itself as an instructive touchstone for our argument. It revolves around Thomas Bruce, the seventh Earl of Elgin and the British Ambassador to the Port of Constantinople (Istanbul), the capital of the Ottoman Empire, which at the time occupied what we today call modern Greece. Between 1801 and 1804, Lord Elgin dismounted huge figures, friezes, parts of columns, and other monuments from the Parthenon – representing more than half of all the surviving sculptures from the Acropolis – and sailed them to London. In 1816, in the immediate aftermath of the birth of the concept of restitution at the Vienna Congress, a Select Committee of the House of Commons debated the legitimacy of Lord Elgin's acquisition from the Acropolis. Despite serious objections, Lord Elgin prevailed and the Parliament came to conclude that the sculptures were legally acquired and properly held. Parliament then decided to buy the sculptures at the recommended price of £35,000 and display them as a unified collection at the British Museum, where they have remained to this day.

This cause célèbre has generated its own body of scholarship, which has predominantly focused on the historical trajectories of the monument (St. Clair, 1998), the justification or not for Lord Elgin's removal of the sculptures in the form of a so-called *firman* (the Sultan's decree; in this case, an official permission from the Ottoman authorities in Athens to remove the monuments), and contemporary arguments pro and con return (Greenfield, 2013 [1989]; Hitchens, 1987; Webb, 2002). Much less has been written about the shifting discourses surrounding the claim, since Greece was recognized as a sovereign nation-state in 1830 and restoration work began on the Acropolis.

The first formal claim to the sculptures was filed through official diplomatic protocols as late as 1983, following a celebrated speech by Melina Mercouri, Greece's Minister of Culture, at a UNESCO summit in Mexico City in 1982. In an eloquent, emotional plea, she called upon Athena, goddess of wisdom "and the very expression of education, science, and culture" (the central "ESC" in UNESCO's acronym), in whose honor the Parthenon temple was built, before adding: "As a Greek, as a woman, and as the representative of the first socialist government of Greece, I am proud that the Parthenon, that temple which has withstood time, wars, occupations, has been chosen as the symbol of UNESCO" (Mercouri, 1982) (Figure 6).

One of Mercouri's first acts upon assuming a cabinet post in Greece's first left-of-center government at the end of 1981 was to raise the issue of the Parthenon sculptures' return. "Since then," she said in her speech in Mexico City:

> a small storm has been raging. But what I find most interesting is the fact that, following an interview with BBC, I had hundreds of encouraging letters from individuals and organizations in Britain. I detect in these letters the English people's love of justice and beauty. After all, the sacrilege of Lord Elgin was immediately condemned at the time, in England itself. . . . I think that the time has come, for these marbles to come back to the blue sky of Attica, to their natural space, to the place where they will be a structural and functional part of a unique whole. (Mercouri, 1982)

Following Mercouri's address in Mexico City, Greece filed a formal claim for the return of the Parthenon sculptures from the British Museum with UNESCO's Intergovernmental Committee for Promoting the Return of Cultural Property to Its Countries of Origins or its Restitution in Case of Illicit Appropriation. The claim was justified with recourse to the three principal ideas foreshadowed in the speech: (I) the aesthetic argument that the sculptures are integral to the monument and genius loci of the Acropolis; (II) the political argument that the sculptures belong to the place and milieu, where they came into being; and (III) the legal argument that the sculptures had been removed

Figure 6 "Because they are the symbol and the blood and the soul of the Greek people." Greek Minister of Culture, Melina Mercouri, visits the Parthenon Sculptures at the British Museum in London. © PA Images / Alamy Stock Photo.

illicitly, without local authorization and from a nation with its hands tied due to Ottoman occupation.

A year later, the British Government responded only to the last part of the claim, which it formally declined on the grounds that the sculptures were "secured" by Lord Elgin "as the result of a transaction conducted with the recognized legitimate authority at the time" (Greenfield, 2013 [1989], p. 87). During her two terms as Minister of Culture, Mercouri continued, however, to campaign for the return of the sculptures with impassioned pleas that referred, ultimately, to the emancipation, the unity, and the sovereignty of Greece:

> Because they are the symbol and the blood and the soul of the Greek people. Because we have fought and died for the Parthenon and the Acropolis. Because when we are born, they talk to us about all this great history that makes Greekness. Because this is the most beautiful, the most impressive, the most monumental building in all Europe and one of the seven miracles of the world. Because the Parthenon was torn down and mutilated when we were under the Ottoman Turkish occupation. Because the marbles were taken by an aristocrat like Lord Elgin for his own pleasure. Because this is our cultural history and it belongs not to the

British Museum but to this country and this temple. . . . The marbles have been in England for 180 years. That's enough; it's time for them to come home. (Mercouri, 1984)

We would be hard pressed to come up with a demonstration that is finer or more appropriate than Mercouri's words of cultural property as a technology of sovereignty; with claims that help to produce sovereign subjects in the mold of the liberal modern state: nations with rights, territories, borders, and property. Throughout the 1980s and 1990s, UNESCO adopted a series of recommendations to encourage bilateral negotiations and ultimately the return or restitution of the sculptures. These led nowhere, but certainly provided a cause around which to rally and unite the Greek nation.

In 2002, however, the directorship of the British Museum changed and so did the response to the Greek claim. As discussed in the opening section of this Element, along with eighteen sister institutions, the British Museum reinvented itself as a "universal museum": housing encyclopedic collections embodying all the arts of all the civilizations, which could only be justly appreciated under one single roof. In the meantime, the Greek claim has caught up, so to speak, with the idea of universalism. Thus, in 1983, the British Museum made the case for

Figure 7 Main Hall at the New Acropolis Museum, which is almost void of objects, but with spectacular vistas to the in situ site of the objects, making a powerful architectural argument for the "reunification" of all the Parthenon sculptures that once endowed the temple. Photograph by Martin Skrydstrup.

retention on the basis of legalities recognized by the (Ottoman) authorities at the time of acquisition. The contemporary Greek claim, as well as the British Museum's current case for retention, is couched in very different terms.

In March 2008, the Hellenic Ministry of Culture and UNESCO convened the *Athens International Conference on the Return of Cultural Objects to their Countries of Origin*, in conjunction with a preopening of the new Acropolis Museum, built specifically to house the Parthenon sculptures currently at the British Museum. The partly empty galleries made it clearly visible that the Parthenon sculptures were "in exile," a turn of phrase from Michalis Liapis, Melina Mercouri's successor as Greece's Minister of Culture (2007–9). Speaking on this occasion, Liapis reiterated the aesthetic claim from 1983 for return as a "re-unification of the Parthenon sculptures." However, according to Liapis, the claim is not made merely as a cultural property claim on behalf of the Greek nation, but "in the name of the world's cultural heritage; a universal demand and a global debt to Greece." The Minister closed his speech by contending that the best supporters for the claim would be the thousands of visitors, who would see the New Acropolis Museum and "will be thinking that some pieces of these artefacts are 4,000 miles away from their destination point" (Conference recording on file with the authors).

Figure 8 Greek Minister of Culture, Michalis Liapis, speaking at the Athens' Repatriation Conference making a new argument for the return based on precedence and the *genius loci* of the site, now offering, for the first time in the history of the dispute, professional curatorial facilities and aesthetic integration with the original site. Photograph by Martin Skrydstrup.

Partly through extravagant expenditure on this event in the shadow and light of the Acropolis, a nation-state asserted its sovereign right. Interestingly, from our point of view, the rhetorical tactics of the claim have shifted from Minister Mercouri's claim for the restitution of cultural property in the course of the 1980s to Minister Liapis' claim for the return of the "world's cultural heritage" as a "global debt" to Greece. After all, the very premise of European Enlightenment thinking upon which the British Museum's appeal to universalism and encyclopedic collections rests is Hellenic.

Nevertheless, although the Greek government deployed the term world heritage in this instance, we maintain that at its core the case still turns on the congruence between the artifacts and the territoriality from which they were removed and involves centrally the production of the sovereignty of the claimant. In other words, claims made under the sign of cultural property produce and assert territoriality and sovereignty, even when they are cast in the language of world heritage.

The Kwakwaka'wakw Transformation Mask

The inauguration event in 2008 of the new Acropolis Museum in Athens closed with a moving case, which projected the same technology of sovereignty couched in the same evocative language of original wholes, scattered parts, and contemporary need for reunification as in the aforementioned Scottish and Greek cases. Partly as a building block to establish a precedent for international voluntary returns and thereby strengthen the case for the return of the Parthenon sculptures, Andrea Sanborn from the Kwakwaka'wakw First Nation had been invited to Athens to present the return of the transformation mask, which was formally owned by the British Museum. This would make the Kwakwaka'wakw First Nation and the Greek nation-state brothers-in-arms fighting a common cause against the same holding institution.

This transformation mask may represent *IMAS*, an ancestral spirit, or *K'_umugwe'*, the Chief of the Undersea Kingdom. The dancer wearing the mask would pull the mechanical rigging, which would reveal a sun or a starfish figure, illuminating transformations. This particular mask was used in a potlatch (ceremonial gift giving) in 1921, which the federal government of Canada had outlawed in 1884 with *The Indian Act* (often referred to as the anti-potlatch law). Collecting artifacts, stories, and myths among the Kwakwaka'wakw in the 1880s, Franz Boas (considered one of the founding fathers of cultural anthropology and folklore studies) recorded the following logic of the potlatch institution: "It is a strict law that bids us dance. It is a strict law that bids us distribute our property among our friends and neighbors. It is a good law. Let the white man observe his law; we shall observe ours" (Chief of the Kwagu't. to Franz Boas, October 7, 1886. Cited in Cranmer Webster, 1992, p. 30).

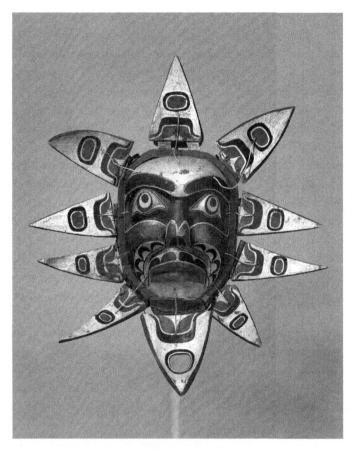

Figure 9 A 'Namgis ceremonial transformation mask of the Kwakwaka'wakw of the Pacific Northwest coast in Canada. The mask was carved around 1910 to dance at potlatches – performative feasts displaying wealth and heirlooms, banned by the Canadian Government in 1884. In 1921, Dan Cranmer on Village Island ('Mimkwamlis) hosted an illegal potlatch, where more than 200 items were seized. The following year, these family potlatch regalia were sold to North American museums. In 1938, one of these museums, now called the National Museum of the American Indian, sold the present mask to Harry Beasley for his Cranmore Museum in Kent. Mrs Beasley donated the mask to the British Museum in 1944. In 2005, the mask was loaned to the U'mista Cultural Centre, at the 'Namgis community of Alert Bay, British Columbia, where it is currently displayed alongside other masks and potlatch regalia returned from North American and European collections. This mask represents an ancestral being of the Kwakwaka'wakw, perhaps the mythic figure K'umugwe', the Chief of the sub-sea Kingdom K'umugwe' (the "wealthy one"). © Trustees of the British Museum.

However, unlike the Chief of the Kwagu't, the federal government of Canada did not subscribe to biculturalism in the first of half of the twentieth century; the federal police considered the potlatch synonymous with the destruction of valuable property. In other words, from the perspective of a protestant ethic and the spirit of high capitalism in Ottawa, the potlatch as an institution of lavish feast-giving was both wasteful and immoral, and moreover a heathen practice that should be suppressed and eradicated by all means necessary.

On December 25, 1921, the Kwakwaka'wakw chief Cranmer challenged this outlawing of the potlatch and orchestrated what some say was one of the most grandiose potlatches ever held on the Northwest Coast in the village of 'Mimkwamlis (Village Island); a remote island about 300 km northwest of Vancouver. Most likely, Cranmer chose the date (Christmas Day) to avoid federal police officials, but nevertheless Indian Agent William Halliday tracked the potlatch and arrested forty-five people: twenty individuals including high ranking chiefs and women were imprisoned, three cases were appealed, and twenty-two individuals received suspended sentences in return for agreeing to hand over their potlatch regalia. Somewhere between 600–750 potlatch paraphernalia (masks, rattles, and family heirlooms) were handed over, for which the Natives received collectively $1,495 from the Federal Government. Anthropologist Ira Jacknis argues persuasively that the Kwakwaka'wakw never forgot this forced appropriation of their regalia (Jacknis, 2000; 2002).

In the decades following the seizure of the potlatch collection in 1921, the collection was split and single pieces entered individual trajectories. The transformation mask entered the private collection of Harry Beasley in the 1930s; a well-endowed Englishman from Kent, who set up the Cranmore Ethnographical Museum. Beasley passed away in 1939 and his collection was then stored at the British Museum during WWII; in 1944, the ownership was formally transferred. *The Indian Act* was quietly dropped in 1951 and the potlatch ban lifted. In 1953, the first "legal" Kwakwaka'wakw potlatch was held and the first recorded efforts to have the potlatch collection repatriated date from 1958 (Jacknis, 2000). The Kwakwaka'wakw, in anticipation and preparation for the return of the collection, successfully raised funds for two cultural centers in which to house the collections during the 1970s, as many holding institutions made repatriation conditional on the establishment of museum facilities to curate the collection according to professional standards. For that purpose, the U'mista Cultural Society was incorporated in 1974. The Society accounts for its name in the following way: "In earlier days, people were sometimes taken by raiding parties. When they returned to their homes, either through payment of ransom or by retaliatory raid, they were said to have 'u'mista'. The return of our treasures from distant museums is a form of u'mista" (U'mista Cultural Society, n.d.).

Native art comes home — and a dream comes true

Andrea Sanborn with the prize she recovered from the British Museum after a long, determined fight.

Mask returns after 80-plus years in U.K.

BY JACK KNOX

ALERT BAY, B.C. — On Andrea

"I've come for the mask," she said, straight-faced. Not only did she go home emp-

the renowned institution have improved dramatically. Sanborn finally saw her dream

Figure 10 Andrea Sanborn poses with the 'Namgis ceremonial transformation mask, as well as other masks in the background, at the U'mista Cultural Centre in British Columbia in 2005. Photograph by Jonathan C. H. King (Press article by Jack Knox, press photograph by Debra Brash

As Ira Jacknis remarks, u'mista is "a perfect Native gloss for repatriation" (Jacknis, 2000, p. 272). Theoretically, this example speaks to the centrality of a notion of agentive objects. The name chosen for the U'mista Society implies that repatriated objects contain embedded agency.

In 1992, seventy years after the initial potlatch confiscation, the National Museum of the American Indian in the United States repatriated nine of the potlatch paraphernalia to the U'mista Cultural Center. This was done unconditionally as a transfer of ownership in recognition of the sovereign status of the Kwakwaka'wakw community, under the sign of cultural property. Throughout the 1990s, however, the British Museum refused to return the transformation mask, but a series of seminars and informal meetings in the early 2000s resulted in the Director for the U'mista Cultural Centre formally asking for a loan of the transformation mask. In February 2005, Neil MacGregor, Director of the British Museum, and Andrea Sanborn began to negotiate, and that same year the British Museum transferred the transformation mask on a five-year renewable loan to the U'mista Cultural Centre, where it was first displayed that same year. Three years later, at the 2008 inauguration conference of the Acropolis, Andrea Sanborn said that such a loan was something that they accepted for the time being and continued:

> Our story begins with the creation of our ancestors in our territories . . . We have come to understand that the very soul of our culture remains fragmented until all the pieces can be reunited, repatriated, and returned home . . . Give us back our cultural ceremonial masks and regalia . . . .Only then can the spirits of our ancestors be at rest, as we will have '*u'mista* and we can continue rebuilding our culture and our lives and become whole again. (March 2008, recording on file with authors)

What we have here is the same assertion of territoriality, sovereignty, and origins, as in the Parthenon case; spiritual wholeness replaces aesthetic integrity. Common cause makes the Greek nation and the Kwakwaka'wakw First Nation contemporary subaltern allies set against the same institution. This alliance between nation-states and First-Nations illustrates the affinities between claim-making as a technology of sovereignty at different scales, enabling new types of alliances across the world.

The ki'i la'au

Extending the analogy to other settler-colonies, NAGPRA (Native American Graves Protection and Repatriation Act, 1990) could be viewed as a machine that produces sovereignty at the subnational level. That is apparent in Hawai'i where repatriation claims are often coupled with notions of "Native Soil," the "Hawaiian cultural renaissance," and the various movements for sovereignty, both royalist and otherwise. The same goes without saying for Native Americans on the Mainland; claims staked through NAGPRA assert and help produce tribal sovereignty in the various configurations ("homelands," "shared sovereignty," and "shared tribal management of repatriation/burial sites"), which Thomas Biolsi (2004) has outlined vis-à-vis the federal government.

The institutional life of artifacts and human remains in Hawai'i revolves around the Bishop Museum, founded in 1889 by Charles Reed Bishop in honor of his late wife, Princess Bernice Pauahi Bishop, the last descendant of the royal Kamehameha family. This marriage between a missionary and a royal sovereign enshrined in a Victorian institution shortly before the Hawaiian monarchy was overthrown in 1893, reverberates in the contemporary political context. Currently, this quintessential Victorian institution is part

Figure 11 The Bernice Pauahi Bishop Museum and Planetarium, designated the Hawai'i State Museum of Natural and Cultural History in the historic Kalihi district of Honolulu on the Hawaiian island of O'ahu. Founded in 1889, by Charles Reed Bishop (1822–1915), an American businessman, and Princess Bernice Pauahi Bishop (1831–84), the couple originally intended the museum to house family heirlooms passed down through the royal lineage of the Kamehameha Dynasty, which ruled the Kingdom of Hawai'i from 1810–72. Today, the institution holds one of the world's most comprehensive collection from the Pacific and is the only one of its kind to house cultural artifacts in the State of Hawaii. Photograph by Mark Miller (CC BY-SA 4.0).

Figure 12 The Museum of Natural History and Planetarium, Providence in Rhode Island, USA. This museum was the repository of the Kii Lau from late nineteenth century to 1996, when the object was "gifted" in a ceremonial exchange at the stairs of the Museum to the Office of Hawaiian Affairs and Hui Malama. Photograph by Martin Skrydstrup.

of the fiftieth State of the United States, set on a lush hill with sweeping views of the harbor and high-rises of the capital of Honolulu. Built in rough textured volcanic black-brownish lava stone with small, blinded windows and a copper roof in a majestic neoclassical architectural style, the building embodies historical legacies. This institution is the only museum in the State of Hawaii with collections of historical and cultural artifacts from pre-Christian times and considered as the premier repository for the cultural and natural history of the Pacific. Its collections span millions of cultural objects, archives, photographs, and natural specimens, which have become increasingly contested under NAGPRA and its current mandate to serve and represent the interests of Native Hawaiians.

NAGPRA only recognizes "Native Hawaiian Organizations" as legitimate claimants, which has led to several contestations about the rightful disposition of human remains and artifacts. These are sometimes referred to as the "artifacts wars" (Johnson, 2007; Jolly, 2017), where the dividing line cutting through the

Native Hawaiian community seems to revolve around preservation vs. reburial of the past. However, this is a much-simplified version of the repatriation scene and the multiple entanglements of objects across institutions in Hawaii. The following ethnographic snapshot of a single object serves to nuance this and show how a single Native Hawaiian claimant performs a technology of sovereignty.

The object in question is a carved wooden piece of about 40 cm in height depicting a human, which, depending on perspective, is referred to as a *ki'i la'au* (wooden figure), a *ki'i aumākua* (a sacred receptacle for a deity), or a supporting figure originally mounted on a chief's canoe to hold spears or fishing poles. The case was disputed in 1996–8 between the keeping institution, the Museum of Natural History and Planetarium in Providence (RI), and the two Native Hawaiian claimants: the Native Hawaiian Organization *Hui Malama I Na Kupuna O Hawaii Nei* and the Office of Hawaiian Affairs (OHA). In the spring of 1998, after two years of dispute, litigation, and court-ordered mediation, the parties reached a settlement, whereby OHA made a donation in the amount of $125,000 to Providence and the Museum donated the object to OHA, which then transferred it to the Bishop Museum.

The following rendition of the case is based on one of the author's (Martin's) fieldwork in the fall of 2006 in Hawaii, where the actors of the case "talked story" (*mo'olelo*), and in Providence, New England, where he conducted a series of interviews with the professionals involved in the case, using a notepad but not a recorder. Here we have tied fragments of their narratives into a case trajectory; the first person singular in this account refers to Martin.

I first met with Halealoha – the *Po'o* (leader) of the Native Hawaiian organization Hui Malama – who picked me up at a small airstrip on the island of Moloka'i. This island has the State's highest unemployment rate and the highest percentage of Native Hawaiians. It is generally considered to be the most "Native" of the eight major Hawaiian Islands. Not surprisingly, this was the island where Halealoha had his homestead. He had invited me here without any advice, apart from a sentence in his email where he said that I would be welcome as long as I understood the ways of Moloka'i.

When we left the airstrip and drove off in his vintage Chevy-pick-up truck he gave me a five-page document and said: "This is what the whole thing is about!" The document was entitled *Repatriation efforts successfully undertaken and supported by Hui Malama I Na Kupuna O Hawai'i Nei*. The first paragraph read: "Over the past sixteen years, Hui Mālama has completed repatriation projects involving *iwi kūpuna* (ancestral bones) and *moepū* (funerary items) held in institutions in Hawai'i, the continental United States, Switzerland,

Canada, Australia, and Scotland. In addition, Hui Mālama has assisted other Native Hawaiian organizations to conduct repatriation. The number of *iwi kūpuna* repatriated total approximately 5,915 individuals and several hundred *moepū*. Disturbingly, in certain instances *iwi kūpuna* identified in museums' records were never located ... The following list provides a year-by-year history of the Hawaiian repatriation efforts completed by Hui Mālama and the efforts of other organizations that we supported." The list contained ninety-six entries of which the Providence case was #59, dated August 1998. It was a comprehensive list, which not only told the story of an on-going campaign, but also the systematics and bureaucratic discipline of its execution. Passing through a stunningly beautiful landscape, I then asked Halealoha how Hui Mālama came into being:

> In 1988, on Maui at a place called *Honokahua*, a private landowner obtained permission to develop a Ritz Carlton hotel. During construction, more than 1,100 *iwi* (human bones) were unearthed, removed, and examined by archeologists. They were of course all *kanaka maoli* (Native Hawaiian). Archaeological osteology – or any scientific testing – is in our view a desecration of the dead. Osteology means that you're extracting *mana* (spiritual power) from the *iwi* (human bones). Archaeologists handle *iwi* without the necessary cultural protocols. We believe that an act, which harms the dead cannot benefit the living.

The road became a little challenging and Halealoha paused for a while, then he continued:

> I was angry and frustrated; we all were. Who had invited the archaeologists to the dinner table! I couldn't wrap my head around the fact that it was their natural right to study other peoples' craniums! You see *iwi* is family; I have never seen a father voluntarily give up his family. It is inconceivable in Hawaii. We wanted the *iwi* returned to their families, we wanted to replant them in Native soil and we wanted to protect our sacred burial sites from intruding archaeologists. However, we did not know how to do *pono* (right, balance, responsibility) to the unearthed *iwi* and we did not have a law to protect our ancestors. This was how NAGPRA and Hui Malama came about.

Here Halealoha somehow hinted at the story circulating that he penned large tracts of the NAGPRA statute, when he clerked as a young attorney in the office of US Senator Daniel Inouye (who was one of the leading protagonists for NAGPRA) and the Senate Committee on Indian Affairs. Be that as it may, the fact that Hui Malama is the only Native entity directly named in the NAGPRA statute does speak to an entangled genealogy of law making.

Figure 13 Hawaii: A signpost of the contemporary sensibilities toward Native Hawaiian sacred sites. Photograph by Martin Skrydstrup.

At his homestead farm, Halealoha confided that the *iwi* (bones) of his ancestors nourished the ground from which the food grows: "When our ancestors are in the ground, where they belong, they nourish our spirits and our bodies," and continued, "You see, I take care of the *iwi* and they take care of me. The relationship between ancestors and their living descendants is one of reciprocity and interdependence. We have a duty to care for the dead. It is our *kuleana* (responsibility). In return, the ancestors give us spiritual protection. I hope my children some day will seed my bones, they will grow, nourish, disintegrate, and return." I realized that the *Po'o* had just conveyed what it meant to be rooted in Native soil on Moloka'i and the cultural rationale for bringing *iwi kūpuna* to their burial places in Hawaii from across the globe. What is striking is that *within* the sovereign subject, we see the exercise of engagement and exchange, as well as reciprocity and responsibility toward the ancestral remains, as an internal regime. This internal regime of responsibility and reciprocity within the sovereign subject is particularly articulated when Halealoha speaks about *pono* (i.e. the Hawaiian term for proper or right):

> The *pono* place for *iwi kūpuna* (human remains) is not on a museum shelf or display or in a lab. It is in Native Hawaiian soil. It was wrong to remove them in the first place. These actions have disturbed the balance of things. By

getting to know how our ancestors are mistreated, we go through and relive anger and frustration, which makes us accept the responsibility of caring for our ancestors, which is a heavy responsibility. Ultimately, it is about *pono* (righteousness/justice).

Following up, I asked him how the Providence case broke: "We got an anonymous fax from somebody in Providence about the intent of the museum to sell the object. That's how it all began," he said, and continued:

> During the public ceremony outside the museum in August [1998], a white lady approached me and squeezed my hand. I had a gut feeling that it was her who sent the fax. Chief Sachem Thomas [from the Narrangansett Indians] helped us throughout, even though he got the flu. Throughout the ceremony we only recognized the authority of Chief Sachem, not the Mayor of Providence. We were on Narrangansett land. We gifted Chief Sachem a weapon.

Here we see how Hui Malama performs sovereignty vis-à-vis Chief Sachem Thomas, and refuses to recognize the authority of the holding institution or that of the Mayor of Providence, "Buddy" Cianci (1941–2016). As a token of mutuality between sovereigns, things are gifted, whereas the transactional modality between Hui Malama and the keeping institution, which is not recognized as sovereign, is monetary. I then asked Halealoha about the specifics of the public ceremony in Providence:

> The night before the ceremony we guarded the *ki'i* (image/man) in our ways [the Hui Malama slept with the figure]. The whole ceremony was about cleansing the *ki'i*. We separated the *ki'i* from the Mayor and his Museum. Officially, the ceremony was an exchange of gifts – OHA donated quilts and dough to the Mayor and the Mayor donated the *ki'i* to us – but the ceremony we performed was all about closure and separation. We never wanted to see the place again. All our protocols and rituals were about eradicating the connection between the *ki'i* and Providence. We performed our traditional recitations to this end and the Mayor thought these were death spells against him and he threatened to sue us for libel. After the ceremony, we just wanted to get home, as fast as possible. We exchanged recognitions with Chief Sachem, but we never recognized the Mayor. After the ceremony, they wanted a press conference in Providence. The Mayor wanted it, OHA wanted it, but Hui Mālama said no. We did not want a horse and donkey show. It's not what it's about.

We see here how a technology of sovereignty is performed vis-à-vis the holding institution, where the ceremony for the Native Hawaiian claimant is about closing, separation, and the eradication of any ties between the object and its erstwhile keeper. Hui Malama performed a ceremony, which was intended to

Figure 14 This is the original entry in the acquisition protocol of the Museum of Natural History and Planetarium defining the Kii Lau as: "E2733: Spear Rest. One of a scant 100 pieces of Hawaiian Culture from pre-Christian days. *E2733 returned to Native Hawaiians in 1998." Throughout the dispute, the Museum maintained the position laid down in the protocol, that the figure was a utilitarian "spear rest" and thus not "sacred" or an "object of cultural patrimony" within the object taxonomy of NAGPRA, as claimed by OHA and Hui Malama. Photograph by Martin Skrydstrup.

cut ties, assert property rights, secure the object, and bring it back to the sovereign homeland.

Shifting the perspective to the keeping institution, the Director of the Museum told me that at the first meeting with the claimant at Sotheby's Auctions in New York City, the claimants showed up in linen skirts and asked her if she was menstruating. If this were the case, she would have to leave the room where the *ki'i la'au* was being stored. As the Director refused to answer any questions about her menstrual cycle, the claimants threw sand at her: "They were really offensive. They put on an act to make us believe that the object was sacred to them. Formally, according to NAGPRA it was a consultation meeting, but in reality it was theatre." Halealoha never confirmed that they had thrown sand on the Museum Director, but he did say that they had brought Hawaiian sand with them to Sotheby's to put around the *Ki'i Lau* to make it feel more at home in New York City.

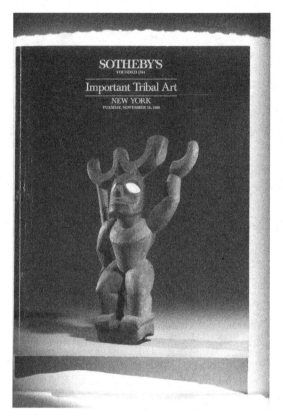

Figure 15 The Museum of Natural History and Planetarium in Providence attempted to auction the *Kii Lau* at Sotheby's in New York City, before the dispute with OHA and Hui Malama broke. Allegedly, an anonymous phone call informing Hui Malama of the intended sale triggered the dispute in 1996. Photograph by Martin Skrydstrup.

After the public ceremony in the summer of 1998 the *ki'i la'au* returned to Hawai'i with OHA and Hui Malama, where it was put on temporary loan to the Bishop Museum and placed in its basement. When I conducted fieldwork in 2006, I asked Halealoha if he was content about the outcome of the case: "Well, I'm glad that we secured the *ki'i*, meaning that it did not end up at some collector's private home, or at Sotheby's in Manhattan. We brought it back to Hawaii." Then I rephrased the question and directly asked him about how he felt about the *ki'i* being in a museum:

> Well, the Bishop Museum is the only repository we have. Putting the *ki'i* into a cave we would run into security problems. The problem is that we happen to live in a society in which a *ki'i* is a precious artifact; that is the

real problem. Otherwise, we could return the *ki'i* to the caves they came from. These objects were not made for aesthetic purposes. You know, when we contemporaries think of a *ki'i* we immediately picture it in a museum context, behind glass in a box with alarms. That is the Western frame of mind. Museums and education is part of Western secular thinking, which they are trying to impose upon us. Repatriation is about the original function of the object. However, in the Providence case we cannot restore the original function to the *ki'i*, because we do not know if it was in a burial cave.

For Hui Malama, the Bishop Museum was the next best thing to restoring the original function of the object and the basement storage almost the functional equivalent of a burial cave. However, this notion of materiality sits oddly with the Bishop Museum's mission to collect, preserve, interpret, and place objects on public display. When I perused the very limited records at the Bishop Museum, I did find plans and sketches for an exhibition of the *ki'i lau* in the aftermath of its homecoming. However, these plans for a new lease on public life for the object never materialized. This is likely because Hui Malama never submitted to reciprocity and responsibility with the new repository (i.e. the notion of cultural heritage as a common regime of knowledge production). Thus, the object sitting in the basement of the Bishop Museum brings out the contrast between the technology of reformation by the Bishop Museum and the technology of sovereignty by the Hui Malama, and ultimately the contrast between cultural heritage and cultural property. With the *ki'i lau* yet to surface from the basement of the Bishop Museum, we might argue that the notion of cultural property has prevailed in this case.

Throughout the case trajectory, Hui Mālama insisted that they are cultural practitioners and that their vocation is the cultural protocols of ceremonial reburials. We have argued that this is a mode of performing sovereignty. This is evident in the larger vision of Hui Malama, which Halealoha evoked at his Father's homestead, explaining that burials nourish the land with *mana* (power/force) and when all the *moepū* (funeral objects) and *iwi kūpuna* (human remains) currently sitting in federal repositories and in museums across the world are back in Hawaiian soil, "Then, we will have our *kulāiwi* (homeland) back." Thus, repatriation is about restoring the lost monarchy, achieving sovereignty and a new future for *Hawai'i Nei* (the Fatherland).

In January 2015, after twenty-six years of repatriation and reburial activities, Hui Mālama was formally dissolved as a nonprofit corporation. Their last act as an organization was to raise funds for a closing ceremony and to pay an accountant to ensure that their tax filings are in order (GoFundMe, 2015).

However, in November 2017, Hui Malama working for OHA was part of the Hawaiian Delegation to repatriate human remains from the Dresden Museum of Ethnology, which had been removed between 1896–1902. At the public repatriation ceremony in Dresden, the museum director Marion Ackermann said that: "Restitution in the field of ethnological museums is often seen as an individual and final act, as an end in itself that could even threaten the survival of the collections and the research of a museum. However, such restitutions should rather be seen as an opportunity that opens doors for joint research projects and cultural cooperation." Thus, the deaccessioning Museum in Dresden attempted to move this repatriation under the sign of cultural heritage. It remains an open question whether Hui Malama shared this notion.

3 Cultural Heritage as a Technology of Reformation

Starting in the 1970s, UNESCO began to develop a separate regime, with its own legal instruments and bodies, for what it calls the safeguarding of cultural heritage (as opposed to the protection of cultural property). Cultural heritage is the preferred term in contexts that stress the general safeguarding (as opposed to legal protection) of artifacts, buildings, sites, and, most recently, cultural practices. UNESCO is today best known in many parts of the world for its Convention Concerning the Protection of the World Cultural and Natural Heritage (aka the World Heritage Convention) from 1972, the associated World Heritage Committee, and especially the World Heritage List. The latter includes such wonders of the world as the pyramids of Giza, Machu Picchu, Angkor Wat, the Great Wall of China, the Roman Colosseum, Stonehenge, Borobudur Temple, Mesa Verde, Notre Dame, and the Acropolis.

Cultural heritage is a concept into which UNESCO itself has breathed life over the past half-century. This concept defines a particular relationship to the objects and expressions it describes, one that is of recent vintage. We tend to assume "cultural heritage" has been around forever; in fact, it is a modern coinage and its current ubiquity limited to the last few decades (Bendix, 2000; Hafstein, 2012; Kirshenblatt-Gimblett, 1998; Klein, 2006; Lowenthal, 1998). Its novelty speaks of contemporary societies and to their own understanding of themselves, their past, present, and future (Eriksen, 2014; Holtorf, 2012; Smith, 2006). Valuing a building or a ritual, a monument or a dance *as* cultural heritage is to reform how people relate to their practices and their built environment, and to infuse this relationship with sentiments like respect, pride, and responsibility. This reformation takes place through various social institutions that cultural heritage summons into being (centers, councils, associations, clubs, committees, commissions, juries, networks, etc.), and through the forms of display everywhere associated with cultural heritage: from the list to the festival – not to leave out the exhibition, the spectacle, the catalog, the website, or the book. Folklorist Barbara Kirshenblatt-Gimblett (1998; 2006) refers to these as meta-cultural artifacts: cultural expressions and practices (e.g. exhibitions, lists, or festivals) that refer to other cultural expressions and practices (carpet weaving, ritual dance, tightrope walking) or material culture (pyramids, cathedrals, masks, chess pieces) and give the latter new meanings (tied, for example, to community, diversity, humanity) and new functions (e.g. attracting tourists, educating visitors, orchestrating difference). A hallmark of heritage, following Kirshenblatt-Gimblett (1998), is "the problematic relationship of its objects to the instruments of their display" (p. 156).

Rather than acknowledging the rights of states, the World Heritage Convention recognizes their responsibilities to current and future generations and to humanity as a whole. In Article 5, states parties are urged "to adopt a general policy which aims to give the cultural and natural heritage a function in the life of the community," while the following Article makes plain their responsibility: "Whilst fully respecting the sovereignty of the States on whose territory the cultural and natural heritage ... is situated, ... the States Parties to this Convention recognize that such heritage constitutes a world heritage for whose protection it is the duty of the international community as a whole to co-operate."

With respect to cultural heritage, UNESCO's regime is thus not rights-based but ethical: World Heritage is designed to mobilize international opinion and to create state practice through moral and rhetorical pressure, dangling the prospect of a place on the World Heritage List before states as an incentive while removal from the List, even the threat of removal, is an effective form of shaming.

If the primary concerns of UNESCO conventions for protecting cultural property are conflicting national claims and the settlement of international disputes over transfer, then conversely conventions for safeguarding cultural heritage organize international cooperation around the common goal of keeping safe and bequeathing to posterity those monuments and expressions that are considered of value to humanity as a whole, regardless of where they are located or who may use them. One way to put this might be to say that under UNESCO's respective regimes, cultural property belongs to an exclusive "us" but cultural heritage belongs to an inclusive "us." In other words, while claims staked within both regimes help to constitute collective subjects, the subject of cultural property is exclusive, subject to misappropriation, and entitled to restitution; the subject of cultural heritage tends rather to be inclusive, a collective "we," which conventions entreat to take responsibility and stand together to prevent degradation and loss, rather than theft by an Other. Compared to cultural property, we might say that cultural heritage is subtler in its perpetuation and its disruptions of state hegemony.

This distinction is clearly recognized by Prott and O'Keefe (1992), who contrast the ownership and exclusivity of cultural property with the responsibilization, custodianship, and sharing that are characteristic of cultural heritage. One is left wondering, therefore, after teasing out the different uses of the two concepts and their associated regimes, why the authors argued for dropping the one in favor of the other.

Of course, the terms are not unequivocal and we should be careful not to reify them. Indeed, their distinction is often blurred, as we saw previously in the shifting language in which Greek claims to the Parthenon sculptures have been couched. As anthropologist Haidy Geismar (2015), has noted, cultural heritage, "like its older sister, cultural property, is a tangle of ideology and expectation; an analytic term and a tool of governance; ... [and] a foundational category for a political economy, the 'heritage industry'" (p. 72). Social actors across the globe participate in new opportunities offered by both concepts, and help to shape new options in markets and politics that have come to be imaginable through instruments such as inscriptions and lists.

But even so, in the international regimes the distinction is fairly clear-cut, and one should not underestimate the importance of these regimes in diffusing a conceptual matrix and shaping local practices. The term cultural property gained universal currency following the adoption of the Hague Convention in 1954, not the other way around, and likewise the proliferation of cultural heritage in recent decades only gained momentum as a result of the adoption of the World Heritage Convention in 1972.

In recent years, intangible cultural heritage exemplifies how international conventions, when successful, can act as catalysts; this term, concocted in the assembly halls of UNESCO in the 1990s, has rapidly gained acceptance following the adoption in 2003 of the convention dedicated to safeguarding it. Its widespread use is in some ways confounding, considering its negative semantics and bureaucratic etymology, not to mention that it is enough of a mouthful that it has in many contexts been replaced with the acronym ICH. And yet in tens of thousands of scattered places all over the world, people now refer to their traditional practices as intangible cultural heritage, or as ICH, and in so doing they make claims that are recognizable with reference to an international regime and validated by a proliferating production of expert knowledge on intangible heritage (Hafstein, 2018).

Participation: Making Communities

Based to a large extent on the World Heritage Convention, the Convention for the Safeguarding of the Intangible Cultural Heritage from 2003 extends the reach of international heritage regimes to a new domain of cultural practices and expressions. With thirty years of world heritage under their belt, UNESCO's member states proved ready to take a much larger step away from state sovereignty over heritage and toward the responsibilization of populations, conceived of in the Intangible Heritage Convention as "communities, groups, and in some cases individuals" and entrusted with identifying and managing their intangible heritage in cooperation with state institutions and experts. Deferring even the definition of its subject matter to the populations that it addresses ("The 'intangible cultural heritage' means the practices, representations, expressions, knowledge, skills . . . that communities, groups and, in some cases, individuals recognize as part of their cultural heritage"; art. 2), the Intangible Heritage Convention testifies to an important development in the regime of heritage. From the reference to the "function" of heritage in "the life of the community" (art. 5) in the 1972 convention, "participation" has come to play an ever-larger role in the discourse and practice of heritage from the 1970s to the present time. The Intangible Heritage Convention of 2003 prevails on states to ensure "the widest possible participation of communities, groups and, where appropriate, individuals that create, maintain and transmit such heritage, and to involve them actively in its management" (art. 15).

Two years later, with the Council of Europe's Faro Convention on the Value of Cultural Heritage for Society, states that ratified undertook to:

> a) encourage everyone to participate in: the process of identification, study, interpretation, protection, conservation and presentation of the cultural heritage; public reflection and debate on the opportunities and challenges which the cultural heritage represents; b) take into consideration the value attached by each heritage community to the cultural heritage with which it identifies; c) recognise the role of voluntary organisations both as partners in activities and as constructive critics of cultural heritage policies. (art. 12)

And in 2011, UNESCO's General Conference adopted the Recommendation on the Historic Urban Landscape, calling on all parties to develop "civic engagement tools" to "involve a diverse cross-section of stakeholders, and empower them to identify key values in their urban areas, develop visions that reflect their diversity, set goals, and agree on actions to safeguard their heritage" (art. 24).

Beginning in the 1970s, a turn to "participation" may be observed in widely disparate fields of policy and practice (Cornwall and Eade, 2010), from urban planning (Cornwall, 2008; Friedmann, 2011; Healey, 1997) and architecture (De Carlo, 1980; Jones et al., 2005) to health (Morgan, 2001) and sustainable development (Botchway, 2001; Michener, 1998), and from environmental protection (Bulkeley and Mol, 2003) to humanitarian action (Hinton, 1995), at international, national, as well as municipal levels. As anthropologist Ellen Hertz notes, the "participatory approach is at the center of a semantic field filled with familiar if vague notions: 'engagement,' 'ownership' and 'empowerment,' are the desired or imagined results of administrative and political processes that range from 'capacity building' and 'consultation' to the use of 'focus groups,' 'lay experts' and 'hybrid forums' in the formulation and application of policy" (Hertz, 2015, p. 25). While deferring to an "unimpeachable political subject – 'the community'" (p. 26), the turn to participation has effectively compelled states and intergovernmental organizations to identify, label, and organize these new subjects as political partners. In the heritage field, this turn to participation is evident in a series of new initiatives and approaches (Cortés-Vázquez et al., 2017; Sánchez-Carretero et al., 2019) that go by names like "public archaeology" (Jiménez-Esquinas, 2019; Richardson and Almansa-Sánchez, 2015), "communitarian archaeology" (Merriman, 2004), "public folklore" (Baron and Spitzer, 2007), "participative mapping" (Risler and Ares, 2013), "participatory museums" (Simon, 2010), and "community heritage" (Hafstein, 2014).

Engaging communities through participatory techniques, heritage regimes reconfigure cultural agency and assist in a "proliferation of the social" (Callon et al., 2002), populating the patrimonial field with heritage communities (and "groups and, in some cases, individuals") charged with identifying and safeguarding their own heritage. In objectifying their practices and expressions as "intangible heritage," for example, through the intervention of experts and administrators deployed from metropolitan centers, population groups are invited to subjectify themselves as communities that identify with their cultural heritage and take responsibility for keeping practices and expressions "safe" from change. Government can then act on the social field through communities and by means of, among other things, heritage policies.

This parallels developments in environmental conservation, where there is widespread preoccupation with community, and programs proliferate that devolve to communities the responsibility for putting environmental policy into practice. Political scientist Arun Agrawal (2005) coined the term "environmentality" to describe this governmental rationality in which communities are interpellated as "environmental subjects": Populations learn to conceive of their habitat as "the environment" and to appreciate the need for its conservation, and – through an infusion of expertise and in cooperation with state, nongovernmental, and intergovernmental organizations – they are charged with administering themselves and their environmental practices (Agrawal and Gibson, 2001; Li, 2001; McDermott, 2001).

In much the same way, the conservation of cultural heritage may be described as a technology of reformation. Teaching people to have a heritage, to value it, and keep it safe is a project of *Bildung* or self-cultivation, fostering new forms of subjectivity and cultivating the capacity for action. It is a transformative process, calibrating people's relationship with their practices and their built environment and, as a consequence, their relationships with one another (mediated through those practices and that environment).

Cultural heritage, in this sense, requires both the intervention of outside experts and the training of local experts. Their task is always in part pedagogic, their goal to reform the practices of local populations and reframe their relationships to their (tangible) habitat and (intangible) habitus in terms of heritage. By means of such interventions, populations learn to conceive of buildings and practices as their heritage and to appreciate the need for safeguarding them from change or destruction. Through an infusion of expertise and in cooperation with state, nongovernmental, and intergovernmental organizations, they are consequently charged with administering themselves and their cultural heritage.

The experts, councils, committees, museums, workshops, awareness raising, and grassroots organizations that the heritage regime summons into being, or summons on site, all help to establish lines of communication between the calculations of authorities and the aspirations of free citizens, to mold the ambitions and shape the desires of the latter to safeguard their heritage of their own free accord and initiative. Appealing to their civic duty and moral responsibility for maintaining a particular alignment between the past and the present, in which strong emotions and identities are vested, projects for safeguarding cultural heritage are thus designed to modify behavior, sensitivities, and ideas about preservation and history.

Conduct of Conduct: Heritage as a Form of Governance

As a technology of reformation, safeguarding is part of the arts of governing by means of what Michel Foucault (1991 [1978]) described in his 1978 essay "On Governmentality" as the "conduct of conduct." The conduct of conduct takes place at thousands of scattered points and requires a profusion of techniques and programs for connecting agendas in political centers to those dispersed sites where operations of power connect with the population and its customs, beliefs, health, hygiene, security, and prosperity (Rose, 1999, p. 18). Foucault refers to this proliferation of programs and techniques as the governmentalization of the state. It encourages an equal proliferation of independent authorities and experts (demographers, sociologists, museologists, folklorists, anthropologists, doctors, psychologists, managers, social workers, and so on) and of fields of knowledge and expertise relating to the population.

Many such techniques for the conduct of conduct belong to what is usually referred to as "culture." With the benefit of governmentality theory, sociologist Tony Bennett has argued that we are equipped to move beyond the two culture concepts – the esthetic and the anthropological – to a third understanding of culture as a specific set of instruments for acting on the social with particular ends in view. In this view, culture as a concept and category is a historical formation that has emerged alongside governmental forms of rule. It constitutes a complex of relations between what were previously considered unrelated practices, forging from these a new effective reality (Bennett, 2003, p. 58). Much as "society" and "the economy" have come to be seen as historical formations emerging out of governmental forms of rule that take the population as their object (Mitchell, 1998), Bennett shows how "culture, too, can be approached as consisting of a range of particular forms of expertise arising out of distinctive regimes of truth that assume a range of practical and technical forms through the variety of programs for regulating 'the conduct of conduct'" (Bennett, 2003, p. 56).

It is customary to account for the prevalence of the "anthropological" sense of culture as a whole way of life over earlier formulations of culture as "the best that has been thought and known in the world" (Arnold, 1998 [1869], p. 8) in terms of a democratic extension of the culture concept. However, when culture is understood historically as instruments for acting on the social, Bennett (2003) argues that "this development presents itself in a different light: that is, as a result of the incorporation of ways of life within the orbit of government and, thereby, the production of a working interface between culture and the social" (p. 59).

As Tim Winter (2015) has stressed, we must recognize cultural heritage as a form of governance, "one that has emerged in the modern era, involving the governance of space, of people, of cultures and natures, of material worlds, and of time" (p. 998). In fact, heritage reorders relations between persons and things, and among persons themselves, objectifying and recontextualizing them with reference to other sites and practices designated as heritage. Heritage assembles previously unrelated buildings, rituals, paintings, swords, jewels, and songs, and it addresses them as something to be safeguarded; that is to say, acted upon through programs, schemes, and strategies carried out and evaluated by experts whose operations connect the calculations of authorities with the desires and ambitions of citizens.

Vimbuza: From Health to Heritage

From Kutiyattam theater in Kerala, and Vimbuza healing in Malawi, to the Jemaa el-Fna marketplace in Marrakech, the recognition of traditional practices as intangible heritage across the globe and their inscription on the Representative List of the Intangible Cultural Heritage has brought into being new collective subjects and institutions to represent them, involving local actors in new capacities, making them responsible for safeguarding the practices and making sure they continue, and in many cases vesting them with power to make decisions that were previously distributed among other social actors or else simply unthinkable before the practices came under the sign of heritage. In Malawi, for example, the Ministry of Culture has "convened an official body, the National Intangible Cultural Heritage Committee that comprises cultural workers, academics, and ethnic association members among others" (Gilman, 2015, p. 214). Moreover, the inscription of Vimbuza on UNESCO's Representative List occasioned the creation of a Vimbuza Healers and Dancers Association of Malawi, which

Figure 16 Vimbuza, Rumphi District, Malawi. Photo: Lisa Gilman

immediately established a code of conduct for its members with the proclaimed purpose of countering "the negative image of Vimbuza caused by inappropriate practice" (Gilman, 2015, p. 206).

In Madagascar, a coordination committee formed to oversee the safeguarding of the woodcrafting knowledge of the Zafimaniry and in parallel an association of Zafimaniry artisans was created, the Fikambananan'ny Zafimaniry Mpiangaly Hazo, to safeguard, promote, and transmit their craft ("Periodic reporting … Madagascar," 2012). And in Vietnam, according to the government's report on safeguarding activities submitted to UNESCO, cultural authorities have invested in the management capacity of preexisting Ca trù clubs to safeguard traditional Ca trù poetry singing and as a result "the number of Ca trù clubs that hold regular practices and other activities and have a growing number of members has increased from 20 to 60" ("Periodic reporting … Vietnam," 2013). In all these cases (and countless others), we are witness to an institutionalization of social relations, a centralization of responsibilities, and the bringing into being of new social actors: centers, councils, associations, clubs, committees, commissions, juries, or networks.

This reformation of the subjects of intangible heritage goes hand in hand with a reformation of the objects of intangible heritage: the practices, representations, expressions, knowledge, and skills to which the 2003 convention refers in its definition. Translation into the language of intangible heritage is subject to generic conventions associated with what we might call the heritage genres. These genres promote the traditional practices and in the process they orient them toward display. Thus, besides forming an association and setting a code of conduct, the safeguarding plan for the Vimbuza healing dance in Malawi includes a new book about Vimbuza, a museum exhibit about Vimbuza, an inventory of Vimbuza practitioners, and, last but not least, the regular organization of Vimbuza dance festivals.

A bit more context: Vimbuza is a popular healing ritual among the Tumbuka in the north of Malawi. Showcased on UNESCO's Representative List of Intangible Heritage, it is part of a larger dance-and-drum based healing tradition (*ng'oma*) found throughout Bantu-speaking Africa. Vimbuza was in many ways an odd candidate for the Representative List; for one thing, it is the only disease that figures on it – for Vimbuza names an illness as well as the cure. By means of traditional rituals, Vimbuza healers diagnose and treat spirit-related illnesses, resulting from spirit possession. The healing dance is one of its principal therapeutic rites. Accompanied by drumming and bells, the dance has an active audience made up mostly of women, who take part in the therapy. They sympathize and display solidarity with the possessed dancer by singing and clapping with more and more intensity, while the dance becomes more and more frenzied, until it reaches its peak and the spirits release their grip on the patient (Gilman, 2015, pp. 201–202).

UNESCO describes Vimbuza in the following words on its intangible heritage website and in its pamphlets:

> Most patients are women who suffer from various forms of mental illness. They are treated for some weeks or months by renowned healers who run a temphiri, a village house where patients are accommodated. After being diagnosed, patients undergo a healing ritual. For this purpose, women and children of the village form a circle around the patient, who slowly enters a trance, and sing songs to call helping spirits. The only men taking part are those who beat spirit-specific drum rhythms and sometimes a male healer. Singing and drumming combine to create a powerful experience, providing a space for patients to "dance their disease." Its continually expanding repertoire of songs and complex drumming, and the virtuosity of the dancing are all part of the rich cultural heritage of the Tumbuka people. The Vimbuza healing ritual goes back to the mid-nineteenth century, when it developed as a means of overcoming traumatic experiences of oppression, and it further developed as a healing dance under British occupation, although it was forbidden by Christian missionaries ... Vimbuza is still practised in rural areas where the Tumbuku live, but it continues to face oppression by Christian churches and modern medicine. (UNESCO Intangible Cultural Heritage, 2008)

Based on fieldwork in Malawi, folklorist Lisa Gilman (2015) has analyzed the inscription of Vimbuza. She found that the principal motive for its nomination seems to have been expediency: Compiling a nomination dossier is an arduous task, but Vimbuza was already well documented in several ethnographic studies. That made life easier for functionaries in the Malawi Ministry of Culture charged with getting something onto UNESCO's Representative List, preferably right away. As Gilman found out, however, local practitioners of Vimbuza by and large do not regard it as cultural heritage at all. To them, it is a medical practice. Several healers whom Gilman interviewed remarked that if the government wanted to take an interest in Vimbuza, it should be through the Ministry of Health, and not the Ministry of Culture.

As UNESCO's description acknowledges, the medical establishment in Malawi is critical of Vimbuza as a healing practice. And in a predominantly Christian country with a strong Pentecostal element, the religious establishment is antagonistic toward Vimbuza. Some call it Satanic (Gilman, 2015; Soko, 2014). Mindful of this, it is rather remarkable that among those whom Gilman found to be most supportive of Vimbuza's recognition as intangible heritage are both fundamentalist Christians and medical doctors. They are pleased to see it recognized and showcased as Malawian heritage – as a dance and as an expression of cultural identity – if that means it is divorced from the ritual setting. As such, Vimbuza figures as heritage, not as habitus (Gilman, 2015).

To invoke again Barbara Kirshenblatt-Gimblett's theorization of cultural heritage, to recycle "sites, buildings, objects, technologies, or ways of life" as heritage is to give these things a new lease on life, not as what they once were, but as "representations of themselves" (Kirshenblatt-Gimblett, 1998, p. 151). As a metacultural practice, cultural heritage points beyond itself to a culture it claims to represent. With Vimbuza, it is evident that this metacultural relation comes at the expense of preexisting relations to the practice, which are medical or spiritual. It stands to reason, therefore, that those Malawians who would prefer to eradicate Vimbuza seem more favorably disposed to its standing as intangible heritage than many of its practitioners.

In Malawi, then, a popular medical practice has become the object of safe-guarding, for which it has no need. As one part of the action plan for safeguarding Vimbuza, Malawi now organizes an annual festival for a disease and its treatment, where the dance is detached from its ritual ends and transformed into pure, metacultural display – where it stands as its own representation (Gilman, 2015). It is not hard to see why some healers with whom Gilman spoke feel that the concept of heritage misrepresents their healing practices. Translating the ritual into intangible heritage functions as a counter-ritual, draining it of its powers and substance, leaving the dance as display, the ritual experts on the festival stage going through the motions, acting as-if, for an audience that is not looking to be healed but rather just looking.

In fact, safeguarding has emerged as the single greatest threat to Vimbuza's continued vitality. It is when Vimbuza is treated as heritage that it becomes endangered; its heritagization seems to prefigure and perhaps to hasten its obsolescence. Vimbuza thus provides an ironic demonstration of the effectiveness of cultural heritage as a technology of reformation: how the regime of heritage reforms people's relationship with their practices, their relationship with one another through their practices, and ultimately the practices themselves.

Kutiyattam Sanskrit Theater: Reforming Relationships

In 2008, when presenting the first Representative List of the Intangible Cultural Heritage of Humanity, Koichiro Matsuura, UNESCO's Director-General, declared his confidence that "with time, this List – designed to give more visibility to our living heritage – will contribute to raising awareness of its importance and instill a sense of pride and belonging to custodian communities" (UNESCO, 2008). The prestige of international recognition that comes with listing is thus designed to elicit the self-recognition of communities as custodians of their own heritage. It is supposed to induce in people a desire to have a heritage and to take care of it; to curate their own practices, or those of other segments of the local population.

Kutiyattam Sanskrit theater, the oldest continuously performed theater in the world, was among the first cultural practices to be inscribed on UNESCO's Representative List in 2008 (but had previously been recognized in UNESCO's Proclamation of Masterpieces of the Oral and Intangible Heritage of Humanity in 1999, a pilot program that helped pave the way for the Intangible Heritage Convention; Hafstein, 2018). The plots relate to the Mahabharata and Ramayana epics and the performance tradition is characterized by "highly emotive facial expressions, stylized movements, and sparse dialogue of chanted Sanskrit" with such "aesthetic elaboration and extension of each moment" that only one act can be performed at a time, lasting ca. three hours on a public stage or "anywhere from five to forty-one days on the temple stage" (Lowthorp, 2015).

As folklorist Leah Lowthorp explains in her ethnographic exploration of Kuttiyattam and the creative reframings that have sustained it within shifting cosmopolitanisms: "In the course of the twentieth century, the system that had sustained Kutiyattam as an elite, temple-based occupation for nearly one thousand years crumbled beneath the artists' feet in a dramatic tide of change that

Figure 17 Kutiyattam. From left to right: Margi Raman as Rama, Kalamandalam Hariharan on mizhavu drum, and Margi Usha as Sita in Surpanakankam. Photograph by Leah Lowthorp.

swept over Kerala and the emerging Indian nation" (Lowthorp, 2015, p. 20). Making good on India's commitment to safeguard Kutiyattam, a national center (Kutiyattam Kendra) was founded in Kerala's capital in 2007 to administer an action plan for safeguarding the theatrical tradition. Moreover, its recognition and listing has led to the founding of four new teaching institutions, the coordination of a Kutiyattam network that holds regular meetings, the organization of public awareness raising workshops and seminars, and to public promotion activities including an annual performance festival, documentaries, and school outreach programs (Lowthorp, 2015).

According to Lowthorp, the most important impact of the recognition is felt in the way Kutiyattam artists relate to their art. In an interview, one of these artists seems to confirm Matsuura's prediction: "The greatest effect was that working artists had an awakening, they found a belief in themselves. That was the greatest. Now we're really proud to be in Kutiyattam. It has gained value" (Lowthorp, 2015, p. 167). At the same time, the recognition of Kutiyattam as intangible heritage prompts increased administration, surveillance, and accountability, shaping the conduct of Kutiyattam performers as well as their social organization. In this, it provides a textbook example of cultural heritage as a technology of reformation, reforming both the subjects and objects of intangible heritage, the practices themselves as well as the practitioners and their communities. Another artist with whom Lowthorp spoke reflects: "Now we have a condition of normal working people. It is good for an office but bad for art" (Lowthorp, 2015, p. 170).

Jemaa el-Fna: Bringing Order

The president of UNESCO's first jury for the Proclamation of Masterpieces of the Oral and Intangible Heritage of Humanity was the renowned Spanish author, Juan Goytisolo. Goytisolo spearheaded an effort in the second half of the 1990s to protect Jemaa el-Fna, a busy marketplace in Marrakesh that is the site of myriad performances – storytelling, snake-charming, fortune-telling, preaching, acrobatics, and musical performances, to name a few (Kapchan, 2014). At the time, the city and its contractors were planning to get rid of the marketplace and kick out the peddlers and performers to make way for a shopping mall and a parking lot. Goytisolo and like-minded intellectuals in Marrakesh enlisted the aid of UNESCO and its "critical gaze" (Foster, 2015, p. 229) to save Jemaa el-Fna. In Goytisolo's analysis, the key to saving the square was to change the relationship of the local population (in particular its wealthier, more powerful elements) to Jemaa el-Fna:

> The bourgeois "society" of Marrakesh looks at the square with disdain and has on various occasions attempted to do away with it because they think it is a symbol of backwardness and decay . . . Well, what we are attempting – and

UNESCO's decision will help us in this – is to change the way that many of Marrakesh's own inhabitants look at the square. So that they feel a justified sense of pride. (Goytisolo, 2002; our translation)

By means of new social institutions and using genres of display characteristic of heritage (lists, festivals, brochures, competitions, exhibitions, school programs, etc.), Jemaa el-Fna has been reformed from a rogue element to a public theater of power and Marrakesh-ness. Existing practices and expressions have become objects of safeguarding. As part of UNESCO's proclamation of Jemaa el-Fna, Moroccan and international experts drew up a ten-year safeguarding plan and local authorities created a special commission to implement this plan, which included an urban planning study, the creation of a research facility, the identification of traditional knowledge holders, and provisions to strengthen the customary law relevant to the square's management (UNESCO, 2001). In addition, an early analysis of the impacts of UNESCO's recognition identified plans for weekly storytelling sessions, prize competitions, festivals, and a fund-in-trust for the benefit of old storytellers to encourage them to transmit their skills to young apprentices (UNESCO, 2002a). A fine idea, this fund was ultimately not created, however, and the resources provided by UNESCO for this purpose were returned (Beardslee, 2016). On the other hand, the governor of the Marrakech medina did take the following measures: "destruction of two buildings unsuited to the popular and traditional aspect of the square, removal of illuminated advertising boards, transformation of streets converging on the Square into a pedestrian zone, reduction of car traffic" (UNESCO, 2002b, p. 7).

The programs and prize competitions in Jemaa el-Fna afford an example of particular ways in which administrative structures turn vernacular practices into objects for the government to act on. The actions taken by the governor demonstrate how habitat and habitus may actively be reimagined as heritage, retaining the association of the square with backwardness, to which Goytisolo objected, but refiguring it as a sign of authenticity. Through such safeguarding programs, local councils, administrators, national bodies, and the international community attempt to act on the social field. Their interventions under the sign of heritage transform cultural space into a resource for administering populations, a resource through which communities can police and reform themselves, so they can conduct themselves in accordance with the way they have been, or will be, trained to see the square (i.e. with "a justified sense of pride").

The *Association des Maitres du ḥalqa*, an inclusive artists' association, formed in 2002, following the first heritage festival organized to display the "heritage arts" on the square, "in part as a way of negotiating collectively over the pay for the festival and anticipated benefits coming from the UNESCO designation" (Beardslee, 2014, p. 276). In addition, several smaller associations have formed on the square, "dedicated to a particular genre or ethnicity – one Berber association, two Aissawa, two with assorted musicians and other performers, four Gnawa, and one of storytellers. Most *ḥlayqiya* [i.e. performing artists] claimed to have membership in an association" (Beardslee, 2014, 266–7; cf. Beardslee, 2016). Thus, intangible heritage has proven an effective technology of reformation in Jemaa el-Fna, as ethnomusicologist Thomas Beardslee notes, "fostering the growing sense the ḥlayqiya have of themselves as being a community – a body that is more readily able to act upon and be acted upon by government than would be a population of ungrouped individuals" (Beardslee, 2014, p. 224).

The story of how Jemaa el-Fna was rescued from the blade of the bulldozer is one of the success stories that UNESCO tells about its efforts to safeguard intangible heritage. The story often ends with the phrase: "And the square is still there," offered as a resolution to the narrative. And indeed it is still there; instead of a shopping center and a parking lot, storytellers and glass eaters still perform to the crowds in Jemaa el-Fna; astrologists and water sellers still hawk their services. Instead of one voice, there are many; instead of sameness, difference. Geographer Thomas Schmitt (2005) describes the story of Jemaa el-Fna "as a *local-global* success story with a happy ending (at least for the time being)" (p. 180).

"And the square is still there." Yet, all is not as it was. Something has happened. It is important to understand that safeguarding is a tool of transformation. It transforms people's relationship to their places and practices, and that transformation also affects the places and practices themselves. The

Figure 18 The Jemaa el-Fna marketplace in Marrakech by day, with a *halqa* (audience circle) around the musicians. Photograph by Krzysztof Belczyński (CC BY-SA 2.0).

square is still there, but a standardized cart on wheels with a traditional look-and-feel is now mandatory for food vendors, a nostalgic design introduced by the *Agence urbaine de Marrakech* in 2005 (Bessmann and Rota, 2008, p. 125; Schmitt, 2005, pp. 188–189). Moreover, the city government agency ordered shops around the square to harmonize their storefronts and use uniform, large, green parasols (Choplin and Gatin, 2010, pp. 26–28). With a ten-year plan, a local commission, weekly storytelling sessions, festivals, competitions, and inventories of performers, Marrakeshi authorities have left no stone unturned in their effort to orchestrate difference, to organize Jemaa el-Fna as a safe cultural space characterized by harmony and a pleasant distribution of colors and sounds and products and services. City authorities and bourgeois society are finally succeeding where before they had failed: in bringing order to Jemaa el-Fna.

In safeguarding the square, they have reformed it. Sure enough, Jemaa el-Fna is still busy with life, still teeming with people selling, buying, performing, watching, listening, taking part, or passing through (Tebbaa, 2010). But fire swallowers and musicians, food stalls and preachers are now – increasingly – each in their proper place. Chaos makes way for order as performances and services are zoned.

Folklorist Deborah Kapchan began her ethnographic work on the square in 1994. Twenty years later, she recalls the changes that came with its proclamation as the intangible heritage of humanity:

Figure 19 The Jemaa el-Fna marketplace in Marrakech by night. Photograph by Krzysztof Belczyński (CC BY-SA 2.0).

> In preparation for the rehabilitation of the square, Moroccan authorities relocated all the herbalists to another, single section of the square; what's more, they were told to cease their verbal performances. Obviously, the cleaning up and "preservation" of Jma' al-Fna in Marrakech required a codification of roles in the square, and since herbalists are not in the UNESCO categories of "storytellers, acrobats, or musicians," their own brand of verbal art was not recognized and was ultimately silenced. (Kapchan, 2014, p. 187)

There is more. As noted, to safeguard Jemaa el-Fna, the Medina governor reduced car traffic and created a pedestrian zone in the streets that converge on the square. These measures may sound helpful to the performing artists, the *hlayqiya*, taking away the noise, smell, and distraction of motor traffic in and around the square. Instead, they proved devastating, especially to the storytellers. Already in 1985, when the Marrakech Medina was added to the World Heritage List, the bus station that had been on Place Jemaa el-Fna moved away. That still left shared taxi ranks on the square, but as part of the governor's measures they too moved from the square as motor traffic through Jemaa el-Fna was more or less closed off. This changed the cultural space of the square, but not as the safeguarding plan intended. In his interviews with storytellers in Jemaa el-Fna, Thomas Beardslee found that they blamed the demise of their trade on the removal of the bus stop and the taxi ranks:

> These storytellers – even more so than musicians, magicians or acrobats – depend on pedestrian traffic, specifically on Moroccan-Arabic-speaking audience members with a bit of time to kill. The presence of these transportation hubs meant that the storytellers had a fairly regular supply of audience members coming from the crowds waiting on buses and taxis. Once they were removed, that supply dwindled dramatically: there is no longer the flood of workers leaving the tanneries in the afternoons, no more daytime traffic and waiting crowds from the inter-city bus station, and no morning and evening rush of workers reaching other parts of the city in shared taxis. (Beardslee, 2014, p. 96)

In 2013, the *hlayqiya* went on strike. An American tourist commenting on TripAdvisor on his visit to Morocco in March that year wrote: "The square was lovely. When I visited the first time, there were tons of people and performers. It was great to be able to interact with them. Unfortunately, on this trip the performers were on strike so they weren't out to be seen" (TripAdvisor User Review, 2013). In Finnair's in-flight magazine that same year, a journalist noted that "tonight this UNESCO World Heritage site is quiet. The spot in the middle of the town square where men recant their ancient stories is now occupied with wide banners. Slogans are written in Berber and Arabic and a cardboard sign in English sums up the protesters' concerns: 'Where are the rights of artists in Djemaa el-Fna ?'" (Palonen, 2013, p. 19). The artists had two principal demands: first, that a commission be set up to investigate what happened to the money that the UNESCO Funds-in-Trust made available and was in part supposed to help support them and guarantee the future of their arts on the square; second, that they regain some measure of control over their square, where they are now, they said, confined to 5 percent of the surface while food carts and merchants occupy 95 percent of it with the blessing of city authorities. After several days and many disappointed tourists, the city government promised to produce a benefits program for the performers (cf. Beardslee, 2016, pp. 95–99). As a technology of reformation, cultural heritage cuts both ways.

4 Different Patrimonialities

This is our principal argument: that while their boundaries are often blurred and there are certainly overlaps and overflows between cultural property and cultural heritage, the two represent nonetheless fundamentally different approaches to subject formation, produce distinct bodies of expertise, and belong to different rationalities of government in the patrimonial field, or different "patrimonialities."

Protecting cultural property is a technology of sovereignty. As such, it forms part of the order of the modern liberal state. Regardless even of whether or not they are recognized within legal regimes of cultural property, claims to cultural property help to form sovereign subjects with their own exclusive cultures and autonomous histories: nations, peoples, tribes, etc. with "uncompromising self-sufficiency and mastership" (to quote Hannah Arendt's characterization of the ideal of sovereignty; Arendt, 1958, p. 234) and agency without any expectation of reciprocation or compensation (to refer to Derrida's reworking of Bataille's theorization of sovereignty; Derrida, 1978).

Conversely, safeguarding cultural heritage is a technology of reformation, cultivating responsible subjects and entangling them in networks of expertise and management. The historical ascendancy of the cultural heritage regime coincides with a shift in political economy, from the liberal capitalism of the modern state to neoliberalism with its projects of responsibilization, its delegation of tasks of governance from the state, and its cultivation of "self-governing capabilities" (Rose, 1996). It is therefore a small step from describing heritage as a technology of reformation to linking the regime of cultural heritage to neoliberal politics and forms of subjectivity (Coombe and Weiss, 2015).

Hence, when Prott and O'Keefe suggested in 1992 that it was time for cultural heritage to supersede cultural property as a term of art, this represents, in our view, a political position that reaches well beyond semantics. One might add that this position points in the direction that UNESCO has been heading since the 1970s, with a focus on developing regimes of cultural heritage with an ever more pronounced emphasis on engagement, participation, bottom-up approaches, and community involvement. Indeed, we would suggest that this is part of a larger turn in governmentality in the past half century.

This larger turn, as well as its inherent contrasts, could be exemplified at the case level with reference to the historical trajectories of cultural property/ cultural heritage in the North Atlantic and on America's Northwest Coast. The transfer of medieval manuscripts from Denmark to Iceland (1971–97) exemplifies the complementarity of these two technologies, where claims, counterclaims and actions move between the signs of cultural property and cultural heritage.

The manuscripts case then delivered a blueprint for the so-called UTIMUT case (1984–2001), which comprised the transfer of more than 35,000 objects from the National Museum of Denmark to the National Museum of Greenland. We argue that UTIMUT embodies the completion of the shift from a technology of sovereignty to a technology of reformation. Unlike the Icelandic-Danish case of the return of medieval manuscripts, the return of these holdings to Greenland from Denmark never entered a courtroom or the house of parliament, and never gave rise to legal action or political motions. Instead, UTIMUT depended entirely on museum expertise provided by archeologists, anthropologists, and other heritage professionals.

Finally, we return to the Kwakwaka'wakw transformation mask and follow its subsequent circulation as it was, first, sent from the British Museum on a long-term "renewable loan" to the U'mista Cultural Centre of the Kwakwaka'wakw Nation in British Columbia, and then sent back on a "return loan" to London. In Section 2, we aligned the Kwakwaka'wakw claim for the return of the transformation mask with the Greek claim for the return of the Parthenon sculptures, arguing that both claims can be understood as a technology of sovereignty. Following up on the mask's fortunes, we argue in this section that in the negotiations for the mask, the British Museum has moved the case trajectory away from the sign of cultural property, framing it instead as a case of cultural heritage; a claim based on sovereignty is countered with an offer of engagement, exchange, and a common project, extending museological networks of expertise and management. We turn now to these different trajectories.

The Medieval Manuscripts: From Return to Partition

A large crowd gathered by the Reykjavík harbor on the morning of April 21, 1971. Twenty thousand people, 25 percent of the capital's population (and 10 percent of the country's entire population), had come to meet the Danish naval vessel that delivered the first two manuscripts: Flateyjarbók and the Codex Regius of Eddic Poetry. At the government's request, businesses, shops, and schools closed to allow people to go in person or to watch or listen to the live broadcast on television and radio (the first of its kind on Icelandic television). A brass band performed the national anthems of Iceland and Denmark while policemen and scouts stood honor guard alongside Danish soldiers. The prime ministers of both countries addressed the public. The return itself took place in a formal ceremony between Danish and Icelandic Ministers of Education, attended by other ministers, dignitaries, and diplomats, and preceded by a concert in which the Iceland Symphony Orchestra performed the "tone poem" Saga Dream by Carl Nielsen, Denmark's most prominent composer. Afterwards, the government of Iceland invited the representatives of the Danish government, parliament, and embassy to a reception, along with 300 other guests, where they shared a meal of lobster and prawns with cocktail sauce, beef tongue and rack of lamb, ice cream and coffee, and yet more speeches celebrated this unique occasion, variously interpreted as a return of cultural property from one sovereign nation to another (Greenfield, 2013 [1989]) or as a gift that enabled the two nations to share their common heritage and develop their special relationship (*Morgunblaðið*, 21 and 22 April, 1971).[1]

The country's largest newspaper, *Morgunblaðið*, published a special edition commemorating the return of the manuscripts. A month prior it had interviewed pedestrians in the city center about their attitude toward the return, which ranged from indifference to joy, and from gratitude to the sentiment expressed by painter Steingrímur Sigurðsson: "We have waited for this a long time. Now that our dream has come true, it should remind us that we are an independent people, shouldn't it? With our own soul. I regard

---

[1] For the sake of full disclosure, we should note that the father of one of the authors (Valdimar) was a deputy in the Icelandic Ministry of Foreign Affairs at the time and among the officials sent to greet the Danish naval vessel on that April morning. Valdimar's mother and older sisters stood among the public on the other side of the railings, as did both sets of grandparents and the entire family (he himself was born a year too late). His parents and one set of grandparents were also invited to the reception that night, where his mother recalls that she was seated between "a man from Icelandic Studies" and "an actor from the National Theater." The former was Jónas Kristjánsson, director of the Árni Magnússon Manuscript Institute and delegate to the expert committee created to oversee the partition of the manuscripts between Denmark and Iceland.

Figure 20 Reykjavík harbor, April 21, 1971. Icelanders gather to welcome the medieval manuscripts home. Photograph by Guðjón Einarsson/ Tíminn. Courtesy of the Reykjavík Museum of Photography.

Figure 21 The moment of transfer: The Royal Danish Navy delivers the first manuscripts (Codex Regius and Flateyjarbók) to the Icelandic police force in the Reykjavík harbor, April 21, 1971. Photograph by Kristján Magnússon. Courtesy of the National Museum of Iceland.

the manuscripts as a symbol of spiritual wealth – the common property of the Icelandic nation" (*Morgunblaðið,* 20 March, 1971, p. 11; our translation). His words were echoed in the speeches of Icelandic politicians and academics the following month.

From the eleventh century onwards, Iceland developed a strong writing tradition, recording on parchment the oral histories of Icelanders and of Scandinavian kings and queens, as well as mythological accounts, poetry, and law. These medieval manuscripts include, most famously, the prose Sagas of Icelanders and the poetic Eddas. The advent of Nordic antiquarianism in the seventeenth and eighteenth centuries aroused great interest in these texts, and instigated collection efforts in Iceland. Iceland had been annexed to the Danish crown in the fourteenth century; the Danish monarch was therefore also the king of Iceland, the Royal Archives in Denmark included Iceland in their remit, and the University of Copenhagen was the only institute of higher learning in the kingdom. Icelandic antiquarian Árni Magnússon (Latinized as Arnas Magnæus; 1663–1730) was Professor of Antiquities at the University of Copenhagen and the secretary of the Royal Archives. He organized a systematic collection effort in Iceland, travelling around the country himself to gather nearly 3,000 manuscripts, which he transported to Copenhagen for research and safekeeping. Some of these were lost in the largest fire in the history of Copenhagen in 1728, along with Magnússon's books and records, but the majority survived and his will bequeathed them to the university upon his death in 1730. In 1760, a royal ordinance created the Arnamagnean Foundation to oversee the preservation and publication of these manuscripts.

The transfer of these medieval manuscripts from Denmark to Iceland (1971–97) featured prominently in Jeanette Greenfields's landmark book on *The Return of Cultural Treasures* (2013 [1989]) as an "outstanding example of a major state-to-state return of cultural property," which Icelandic editorial opinion hailed as "a unique step in Nordic and world history – an example and incentive for the rest of the world on how to resolve sensitive disputes" (Greenfield, 2013 [1989], p. 46). This case spans several decades, from the first official requests in the 1930s to a political agreement in 1961 about a partition of the collection, followed by two court cases in the Danish Supreme Court about constitutional breach and compensation to the holding institution. Then, in 1971, the first two manuscripts were handed over to Iceland as "priceless gifts." While this was a day of celebration in Iceland, complete with a brass band, honor guard, and a public holiday, in Denmark the holding institution flagged at half–mast to signal its dismay with Danish politicians as the final arbitrators of the case.

Figure 22 The two manuscripts, Codex Regius (small book) and Flateyjarbók (two large tomes), at the ceremony in Háskólabíó in Reykjavík on April 21, 1971. Photograph by Guðjón Einarsson. Courtesy of the Reykjavík Museum of Photography.

Like the Parthenon, the case has generated its own bibliography (Davíðsdóttir, 1999; Hálfdánarson, 2003 and 2015; Kjær, 2002; Nebelong, 2002; Ólason, 2002; Prott, 2009, pp. 343–46; Sigurðsson and Ólason, 2004), but what is significant for our argument here is that the Icelandic claim for archival materials in the course of the first half of the twentieth century falls squarely within the technology of sovereignty, as a cultural property claim for everything Icelandic held by Danish institutions (manuscripts, documents, letters). More specifically, the case trajectory begins with a request in 1837 for archival documents, asserted again in 1907 and in 1925. In between, Iceland gained home rule in 1904 and Denmark formally recognized Icelandic sovereignty in 1918. The substantial claim for all medieval manuscripts in the holdings of the former colonizer is then articulated in 1930 by a sovereign government on the occasion of the 1,000-year anniversary of the Icelandic parliament, the sovereign body. The demand for the return "home" of Árni Magnússon's collection was reiterated in 1938 on the twentieth anniversary of Iceland's sovereignty (Hálfdánarson, 2003, pp. 181–182).

Denmark's occupation by Germany during WWII interrupted the negotiations and the Republic of Iceland was founded in 1944. In the postwar years, the case took on certain urgency in both countries and became an object of domestic debate in Denmark, which more or less pitted progressive liberals (*kulturradikale*) in favor of repatriation against conservatives and academics advocating retention. Roughly, the former argued for return on the basis of moral rights and Nordic solidarity and the latter were against return with recourse to the loss for science, the legitimacy of the acquisition, and the lack of international precedent (Davíðsdóttir, 1999).

These debates sparked an intricate process, which culminated in a Danish proposal to Iceland for the partition of the collection according to scholarly criteria of provenience and the idea of "common stewardship" of the collection. However, to Icelanders in the mid twentieth century, the only acceptable outcome was that all medieval manuscripts would be returned to an independent Iceland. The proposed "common stewardship" over what they considered their exclusive cultural property did not sit well in postcolonial Iceland; recall Hannah Arendt's characterization of the modern ideal of sovereignty as "uncompromising self-sufficiency and mastership" (Arendt, 1958, p. 234). In 1959, the Icelandic Parliament charged an expert committee with arguing the Icelandic cause and at the beginning of the year in 1961 Iceland's Minister of Education delivered to the Danish Government an inventory that this committee had drawn up containing all manuscripts by Icelandic authors/scribes, suggesting that these be returned. The suggestion was not well received; the inventory included the vast majority of manuscripts in Árni Magnússon's collection.

In the spring of 1961, the parties eventually reached an agreement, which led to the adoption of a law in Danish parliament that circumvented the question of ownership, but instead introduced the notion of "Icelandic cultural heritage." The parties agreed to form an expert committee, charged with partitioning the collection according to a set of criteria of what constituted "Icelandic cultural heritage": based on subject matter, those manuscripts that primarily concerned Iceland would be returned, and those that dealt with other nations retained, regardless of who wrote them and where.

The manuscripts that met the criteria were transferred to the Árni Magnússon Manuscript Institute in Reykjavík, newly created for this purpose and named for the same antiquarian collector as the Arnamagnean Institute in Copenhagen, a sister institute that houses most of the manuscripts still in Denmark. Scholars and technicians at the new Árni Magnússon Manuscript Institute, by and large trained at the Danish Arnamagnean Institute and the University of Copenhagen, were charged with curating and administering the manuscripts after their arrival in Iceland, and special travel grants and scholarships were set up to encourage exchange and cooperation between the sister institutes.

Viggo Kampmann, Denmark's Prime Minister in 1961, remarked in a retrospective interview on the occasion of the first return in 1971, that, "As

I saw it, the return of the manuscripts was in a way a recognition of Iceland as a sovereign nation, but the most important issue to my mind was that returning the manuscripts was an act of friendship by Danes toward their brother nation" (*Morgunblaðið*, 21 April, 1971, p. 10; our translation). His Minister of Education, Helge Larsen, expressed a similar view in the speech he gave as he handed over the Codex Regius and Flateyjarbók, the crown jewels in the medieval manuscript collection at the ceremony in 1971:

> Flateyjarbók came to Copenhagen in 1656, the Codex Regius in 1662, both as gifts to Fredrik III, the first absolute monarch of Denmark. It was a part of absolute monarchy that the state jewels were collected at the seat of the monarch in Copenhagen. Many other manuscripts came later from Iceland to the kingdom's capital and they were preserved there. Absolute monarchy was normal and correct according to the views of that time. In the 19th and 20th centuries, another political ideal prevails, not of centralization but its opposite, the recognition of national and popular rights and sovereignty. It is this leading ideal of the 20th century that we put into practice today with respect to Iceland's request for the return of the manuscripts. At last that concludes a long debate and concludes it according to the demands of our time. (*Morgunblaðið*, 22 April 1971, p. 12; our translation)

Larsen added a caveat, however: "Icelanders get the manuscripts back, but Icelanders will not have their cultural value to themselves . . . All these centuries ago, they created spiritual valuables that have become the common property of Nordic peoples and of humanity as a whole" (*Morgunblaðið*, 22 April 1971, p. 12; our translation).

From 1972 to 1983, the expert committee convened forty-one times to resolve issues relating to the partition. Their work came to an end in 1997, when the last manuscripts were transferred and Iceland signed a protocol in which it accepted that the case was closed. No further requests could be made. In 2009, UNESCO inscribed the Arnamagnæan Manuscript Collection on its Memory of the World Register as the "documentary heritage" of Denmark and Iceland, following a joint nomination prepared by the Árni Magnússon Institute in Reykjavík and the Arnamagnæan Institute in Copenhagen.

The UNESCO inscription marks the culmination of a case trajectory that shifts over the course of a century from a technology of sovereignty to a technology of reformation; that is, from a sovereign claim for the return of exclusive "cultural property" to a partition of the collection, which is associated with the infusion of expertise and institution building around the notion and definition of "cultural heritage." Although the Icelandic government officially accepted the manuscripts as gifts, the local interpretation of their transfer is still very much under the sign of cultural property; as the return to a newly sovereign people of its rightful property from a former colonial ruler (Hálfdánarson, 2015).

The diplomatic genius of the solution was to marry the principle of cultural property – exclusive property belonging to a sovereign people – with the principle of cultural heritage – inclusive and shared, partitioned between the two claimants in a way that ties them more closely together, creating permanent mechanisms for engagement. The definition of "Icelandic cultural heritage" was the key to this solution: it allowed the Icelandic government to claim success in bringing back the nation's cultural property and, crucially, that the "Icelandic cultural heritage" was returned in its entirety. The definition narrowed the scope of the cultural property claimed to those manuscripts only whose subject matter dealt with Icelanders; these effectively represented half the collection (manuscripts written by Icelanders in Iceland) that Iceland originally claimed. When he accepted the first two manuscripts from his Danish counterpart, Iceland's Minister of Education, Gylfi Þ. Gíslason, expressed his gratitude with these words: "You have accomplished a feat. You have treated a small neighboring nation in a way that will never be forgotten. You have set a precedent for the nations of the world to follow, which the history of the world will preserve" (*Morgunblaðið*, 22 April 1971, pp. 1/19; our translation).

The UTIMUT Case

This trajectory of the manuscripts case exemplifies the complementarity of these two technologies of governance. The Icelandic case then delivered a blueprint for the so-called UTIMUT case (1984–2001), which comprised the transfer of more than 35,000 ethnographic and archaeological objects from the National Museum of Denmark to the National Museum of Greenland, according to curatorial criteria worked out between the two institutions (Pentz, 2004). Exported to Copenhagen over the course of three centuries since 1721 (when Danish missionaries set up a royal colony in Greenland), the total number of Greenlandic artifacts in the National Museum of Denmark is still estimated at around 100,000 after the UTIMUT transfer; the world's most comprehensive Arctic collection.

Unlike the Icelandic case, no formal political or legal claims were ever raised in the Greenlandic case. However, piecing together the genealogy of UTIMUT, one finds a first tentative claim from the colony on the metropolis from 1913. Two years earlier, the director of Denmark's National Museum had requested that the Administration of Greenland take appropriate steps to preserve cultural relics against rampant looting of graves, as the museum was entitled to any artifacts discovered. Taking this request up at the 1913 meeting of the Council of South Greenland under an agenda item named "Declaration concerning the

Figure 23 The Umiaq (women's boat) at the Greenland National Museum and Archives in Nuuk. This boat was found in 1951 in Peary Land by Eigil Knuth and excavated and transported to the National Museum of Denmark in 1954. It was one of the key objects of the UTIMUT transfer of approximately 35,000 objects from Copenhagen to Nuuk between 1988–2001. Photograph by Martin Skrydstrup.

Administration's Proposal to Preserve old Cultural Relics in Greenland," the Danish Governor of Greenland suggested that an appropriate response could include founding a Greenlandic museum. Delegates on the council concurred: "We Greenlanders do not havĕ any other history than what can be found in our graves." While agreeing in principle with Copenhagen's proposal to preserve these cultural artifacts, the Council suggested amending the proposal with an additional stipulation: that Greenlandic relics would be banned from export until they had been offered to the (anticipated) Museum of Greenland (*Beretninger og Kundgørelser 1913–1917*, 1914, p. 195). The following year, the Council agreed furthermore to support such a museum financially and to cover all expenses, including for the acquisition of artifacts (*Beretninger og Kundgørelser 1913–1917*, 1915, p. 207). This sent a clear signal to Copenhagen that the Council was serious.

The response from the capital came in codified form as the "Ordinary Circular of April 19th, 1916, from the Secretary of the Interior concerning Measures for the Safeguarding of Cultural Relics in Greenland." This Circular gave the National Museum of Denmark full monopoly on the excavation of

Greenland and permitted export of artifacts from Greenland only via Copenhagen, contingent on their inspection by the National Museum, "which retains the right to keep what is deemed necessary to complete the relevant collections." Moreover, should a museum ever be founded in Greenland to exhibit cultural objects, the "National Museum of Denmark assumes sole responsibility for the selection of such objects" (*Beretninger og Kundgørelser 1913–1917*, 1916, p. 424; our translation). Thus, Denmark categorically over-ruled the first tentative claims, as the National Museum of Denmark asserted

Figure 24 National Museum of Denmark at Frederiksholms Kanal in Copenhagen. This classical Rococo building is still designated "The Palace of the Prince" (Prinsens Palais) by the employees. It was built in 1743 by order of the King Christian VI by Danish Architect Nicolai Eigtved after French ideals. It served as private residence for Prince Frederik V and Princess Louise for a few years. The museum houses what is considered the world's oldest ethnographic collection, established in 1849. Photograph by Martin Skrydstrup.

and maintained absolute authority over Greenland's material past and absolute property rights in any object coming out of the ground in Greenland.

The Circular of 1916 silenced further claims for almost four decades and put to rest, for the time being, all plans for a museum. However, in 1954, in the immediate aftermath of Greenland's formal change of political status from a North Atlantic colony to a dependent state within the Commonwealth of Denmark (which gave Greenlanders Danish citizen rights and two seats in the Danish Parliament), the Administration of Greenland received a letter from a local reverend, Otto Rosing, reviving the museum question: "In these times of change," he wrote, "there is one thing that seems neglected: The establishment of a Museum in this country."

Rosing offered a three-tiered argument for a Greenlandic Museum: first, identity building: "It is hardly surprising that the younger generation seems rootless missing the strength to assert themselves as 'Greenlanders,' when they have completely lost the connection with their skillful and proud ancestors"; second, appropriation and the consequent cultural deprivation: "Our people will become 'poor patriots' if action is not taken now ... we Greenlanders living today are completely ripped of everything – lock, stock, and barrel – of old finds and the like of national value. Everything ended up in Copenhagen"; third, overflow and excess in the capital: "I am inclined to assume, that the National Museum of Denmark will hand over many, many things to our museums up here, if we ask them politely. The National Museum of Denmark must dispose over a lot of things, which they do not have room for and which maybe are just tucked away in the basement ... one might imagine that the National Museum of Denmark would be happy to be relieved of many things, which we could benefit from up here" (Archives of the National Museum of Denmark [Etnografisk samlings beretning-sarkiv], journal #124; our translation).

The Chief Administrative Officer of Greenland forwarded Rosing's letter to the National Museum in Copenhagen. While the response was not unsympathetic, it was unambiguous about questions of authority and control: "The possibility might exist that we could hand over a few duplicates to a future museum in Greenland," they wrote, hastening to add, "We do not possess as many duplicates as one might imagine." Furthermore, "we must insist that the Greenlandic museums should be recognized as provincial museums vis-à-vis the National Museum of Denmark; from which follows that pieces of scientific value must always arrive to and remain in the collections of the National Museum of Denmark." (Archives of the National Museum of Denmark [Etnografisk samlings beretningsarkiv], journal #124; our translation)

It took a decade, but, in 1966, Greenland successfully established its own "Provincial Museum," housed in the Moravian Brethren Mission House in

Nuuk. Representatives of the National Museum of Denmark attended the inauguration and brought as gifts two artifacts from the Danish collection, oddly enough a man's and a woman's dress from Netsilik Inuits in Arctic Canada (collected by Greenlandic-Danish polar explorer, anthropologist, and folklorist, Knud Rasmussen). The Director of the National Museum of Denmark accompanied the gift with good wishes, expressing his confidence "that the Museum will contribute to the safeguarding of the cultural heritage, which the people of Greenland shares with its kinsmen to the West." Six years later, in 1972, with expert advice and support from the National Museum of Copenhagen, the Provincial Museum was upgraded to a Regional Museum, and in 1980 it became the National Museum of Greenland. This trajectory of heightened state recognition may in fact be seen as a function of intensified collaboration, training, and staffing by the National Museum of Denmark during this period. It is clear that the latter institution and its specialists had great use for the museum in Nuuk as a platform for the continued ethno-archeological survey and excavation of Greenland; an institutional gateway to research access.

In 1976, the correspondence between Nuuk and Copenhagen took on a new urgency. Many letters from this year carry the stamp "Urgent" or "High

Figure 25 The Greenland National Museum in Nuuk hosting the 35,000 objects transferred from the National Museum of Denmark, making it the host of one of the most comprehensive transfers of cultural objects the world has seen.
Photograph by Martin Skrydstrup.

Priority." This urgency can only be associated with the parallel exchange relation in the North Atlantic, between Copenhagen and Reykjavík: the manuscripts case. In a letter to Greenland's Chief Administrative Officer, the curator of the polar collection at the National Museum of Denmark, Jørgen Meldgaard, recommended as follows:

> The establishment and organizing of a system of museums in Greenland, facilitated by a museum consultant, who can advise and enlighten about the standards of Danish museology in general and inspire to particular Greenlandic modes of museology . . . We will without doubt be able to handpick competent people in Denmark to professionalize these museological tasks in Greenland. (Letter from Meldgaard to Kontorchef Reventlow, Ministeriet for Grønland, June 23rd 1976, Archives of the National Museum of Denmark [Etnografisk samlings beretningsarkiv]; our translation)

In August 1976, an MP of the Regional Assembly in Nuuk, Otto Steenholdt, brought a motion for an investigation of a possible transfer of "Greenlandic cultural values" back to Greenland. In the ensuing debate, MP Steenholdt entertained the possibility that Greenland might, "like the Icelanders, have to take more radical steps to get these things back." Referring to the precedent set by the transfer of the medieval manuscripts from Copenhagen to Reykjavik triggered a chain reaction through the state apparatus in Copenhagen. On August 27, 1976, Steenholdt's motion was forwarded to the Ministry of Greenland, which on September 7th forwarded it to the Ministry of Culture, which on September 20th forwarded it to the Board of Directors of the National Museum of Denmark, which on September 23rd forwarded it to the Ethnographic Department, where it landed at the desk of Jørgen Meldgaard as curator of the polar collections. The pacing of this correspondence through the metropolitan administration speaks to the urgency of the matter. Well arrived to Copenhagen, Steenholdt's motion set off a race to produce an official position on the matter, which had to reach Nuuk before the motion might be elevated to *realpolitik* in the fall session of the Regional Assembly. Thus, potential claims were dealt with on a proactive and preemptive basis by the metropolitan regime.

On September 30th, Meldgaard penned an official position statement for his department and an internal memo to the museum's Board of Directors: "The Ethnographic Department holds very comprehensive collections from Greenland. The position of the Ethnographic Department is that it would be both natural and fair to transfer collections to Greenland to the extent that Greenlandic institutions and museums find it warranted." Bypassing the administrative apparatus in Copenhagen, Meldgaard sent a copy of this statement directly to the Regional Museum of Greenland, addressing the potential claimant with the following words:

We think it is important that Godthaab [i.e. Nuuk] is briefed as soon as possible about our position. The fall session of the Regional Assembly ends in a couple of weeks ... it would be most unfortunate if Nuuk perceives our attitude to Steenholdt's motion as negative; after all it is our Department which possesses the objects in question. I have enclosed our response, which I trust you will find gratifying.

In his internal memo to the Board of Directors, Meldgaard informed them that:

The Committee for Home Rule in Greenland has mentioned museums among the entities which should be entirely governed by future democratic institutions in Greenland. Otto Steenholdt's motion in the fall session of the Regional Assembly talks about "guarantees, which should be issued about the transfer of values to Greenland, when adequate room is made for these." Steenholdt is also a member of the Committee for Home Rule in Greenland. After having issued our position statement reflecting the very positive attitude of the National Museum of Denmark, we should aim for an agreement, which does not bind us to any detailed blue-print for the allocation between the Danish and Greenlandic parties ... Some Greenlandic cultural treasures and other exhibition-worthy objects will probably be requested by our counterparts in the near future. But the shipment of more comprehensive collections to Greenland should be envisioned in the longer run and the arrangements about scheduling of these transfers, their nature, and extent should be worked out in praxis between the National Museum and the Greenlandic museum system within the frame of a mutual agreement. (Letter from Meldgaard to the Board of Directors, September 30, 1976, journal #2112, Archives of the National Museum of Denmark [Etnografisk samlings beretningsarkiv]; our translation)

Thus, in 1976, Meldgaard conceived the baseline for what would later be designated as the UTIMUT project. The signature feature of the curator's cunning maneuver is the preemptive conversion of a potential political claim into museological cooperation, between Copenhagen and Nuuk. In our terms, the maneuver moves the claim for return of cultural artifacts, set forth in Greenland's Regional Assembly, from the sign of cultural property to the sign of cultural heritage. This feature would become a hallmark of UTIMUT.

However, the Board of Directors overruled Meldgaard's proposal in one regard: "the cultural and historical values of Greenland," he had proposed in his memo to the board, "should be recognized as the property of the people of Greenland. Thus, the Ethnographic Department finds it reasonable that it is left to the democratic institutions in Greenland and a Greenlandic system of museums to be the judge of what objects from the collections in Copenhagen should return home and at which times" (Archives of the National Museum of Denmark [Etnografisk samlings beretningsarkiv]; our translation). At its meeting three weeks later, the Board found "it reasonable, provided certain conditions are met, to surrender parts of its

Greenlandic collection to Greenland," these conditions being an increase in museological skills and competence, storage and preservation facilities, and professional staffing. The board overrode, however, the principle that the collections are the property of the people of Greenland and the deduction that it was therefore up to Greenlanders which artifacts would be returned and when. Rather, the board agreed, "when the above conditions have been met the National Museum of Denmark is willing to negotiate about what kind of objects possibly could be surrendered to museums in Greenland" (Letter from the Board of Directors to the Ministry of Cultural Affairs, October 19, 1976, journal #704, Archives of the National Museum of Denmark [Etnografisk samlings beretningsarkiv]; our translation). We see here how the rationalities of cultural property and cultural heritage are being contested within the same institution; the Department of Ethnography argues for the sovereign rights of Greenlanders to their cultural property but the Board of Directors overrules this and moves the transfer of objects to the sign of cultural heritage, focusing on capacity building and infusion of expertise.

Following a referendum in 1979, home rule transferred various political and fiscal powers to Greenland. The Regional Assembly in Nuuk, where MP Steenholdt brought the motion for an investigation of a possible transfer of "Greenlandic cultural values," became the Parliament of Greenland and at the same time the Regional Museum became the National Museum of Greenland. It is in this political context of Home Rule that the UTIMUT transfer unfolded, between 1982 and 2001, remaining all the while strictly within the museum sector; a result of cunning curatorial expertise. Greenland had to meet a number of conditions with regard to professional standards before the National Museum of Denmark would consider any deposits or returns of artifacts. The metropolitan center then facilitated curatorial capacity building in Nuuk. After these infrastructures had been put into place, the UTIMUT project of return could commence. Significantly, the UTIMUT project gave rise to a new Research Center on Greenland (*SILA*) established in the year 2000 at the sending institution in Copenhagen. In connection with the return of the last object in June 2001, a binding document was signed, which set out the regulations for continuous collaboration and mutual access to the divided collection (Pentz, 2004).

It is instructive to contrast the curatorial conditions and contractual regulations that came with the objects – the conditionality of the return – with Carl Schmitt's characterization of sovereignty as the exception to rules (Schmitt, 2005 [1922]) (or Giorgio Agamben's corollary, that sovereignty is, in fact, indistinguishable from a permanent state of exception; Agamben, 1998). The sovereign has the unconditional ability to transcend rules, a capacity that Greenland signs away as part of UTIMUT.

In a jointly penned article, the two museum directors at the time state that: "This continued cooperation between Denmark and Greenland in the museum field expresses the recognition that the return of the quantities in question involves an obligation for both parties" (Rosing and Pentz, 2004, p. 29). In 2007, Greenland's National Museum and Archives hosted an international conference in Nuuk on the repatriation of cultural heritage, inviting indigenous representatives and museum professionals from around the world and offering UTIMUT as a model of success. The proceedings were published the following year as *UTIMUT: Past Heritage – Future Partnerships* – a telling title. In her introduction (titled "From Conflict to Partnership"), Mille Gabriel of *SILA*, the Greenland Research Center of the National Museum of Denmark, underscores that: "The message of this book is that such partnerships must be formed in a spirit of reconciliation and equitable exchange and, apart from actual repatriation, can include approaches such as knowledge sharing, capacity building, co-curation and co-management of collections" (Gabriel, 2008, p. 13).

UTIMUT thus turns out to be a revealing example of how the technology of reformation responsibilizes and helps to form a new Greenlandic subjectivity,

Figure 26 Entry to the so-called "Repatriation Hall," which was a temporary exhibition by the Greenland National Museum in Nuuk to mark the transfer of the last cache of objects as part of the UTIMUT project, which opened in conjunction with the event "The Conference on Repatriation of Cultural Heritage" hosted by the museum in February 2007. Photograph by Martin Skrydstrup.

teaching the Greenlandic people how to have a heritage, how to value it and how to care for it in particular ways that instill mutual "obligations" on both nations. More generally, UTIMUT embodies the completion of the shift from a technology of sovereignty to a technology of reformation – although this shift oscillates even within the departments at the holding institution in Copenhagen. This shows, for example, in the fact that the Greenlandic case – in contrast to the Icelandic one – never became the subject matter for legal action or parliamentary debates and motions. UTIMUT remains throughout confined to ethno-archaeological expertise within museum networks; a matter of shared cultural heritage rather than exclusive cultural property.

Transformation of the Kwakwaka'wakw Transformation Mask: Curatorial Cunning

In February 2017, the transformation mask was back in London, now subject to a "return loan" from the U'mista Cultural Centre, to which it had been transferred as a "renewable loan" in 2005. Earlier, we argued that the claim for this mask was aligned with the Greek efforts to reunite the Parthenon sculptures (see Section 2) as a technology of sovereignty. However, in the course of negotiating with the U'mista Cultural Centre, we shall argue that the holding institution has turned the case trajectory from a technology of sovereignty to one of reformation. The formal ownership of cultural property is evaded and both holding institution and claimant are enrolled in a regime of engagement (Thévenot, 2015) about the cultural heritage of the Pacific Northwest Coast as a common project of knowledge production for the benefit of the public.

This shift is evident in the exhibition of the transformation mask in London entitled *Where the Thunderbird Lives: Cultural Resilience on the Northwest Coast of North America* (on display at the British Museum in 2017), where the mask embodied the rich cultural heritage of the Kwakwaka'wakw:

> The vibrant culture of the Pacific Northwest Coast is underpinned by power, environment, kinship and interaction. Displayed in the middle of the exhibition will be treasured objects that immortalise these shared core values, including the precious and honoured Potlatch objects. Copper shield shaped sculptures are gifted during an opulent and elaborate ceremonial feast, which are held by powerful chiefs to reaffirm social status and denote the wealth of the hosting family. *Where the Thunderbird Lives* reveals the stories and histories behind these works of art that have united generations and provided stability in the face of great change.

This broad canvas of Pacific Northwest cultures as contemporary, alive, and vibrant represents a radical shift compared with the 1920s, when the mask was seized. However, the notion of *U'mista* (spirited agentive objects) is not fully recognized by the British Museum, which foregrounds instead exchange, reciprocity, and knowledge sharing in its exhibition of the transformation mask: "Most of the regalia has now been returned to the KwaKwaka'wakw and is displayed in community cultural centres. This object has been returned to the British Museum from long-term loan at the U'mista Cultural Centre for this exhibition."

How did this "cunning of curation" (with a nod to Povinelli's argument in *The Cunning of Recognition*; Povinelli, 2002) on the part of the holding institution, shape and ultimately transform the case trajectory? To answer this question, we have to understand the larger change in how metropolitan museums altered their relationships with what they call "source communities" in the past decades. Throughout the 1990s, the British Museum had dealt with the campaign for the repatriation of the Potlatch Collection from various Native constituencies in Canada in the same way as all other requests, by referring to the British Museum Act of 1963 and the British Museum Act (Amendment) Bill. This statute makes it clear that no artifacts in the British Museum can be deaccessioned unless they are duplicates or deemed inappropriate for the museum. This legality overrides all other concerns and considerations, be they ethical, moral, political, or otherwise.

In the 2000s, two events changed this curatorial practice at the British Museum. The first was the enactment of *The Human Tissue Act* (2004), which stipulated the return of human remains and associated objects within certain parameters (e.g. the remains must be less than a thousand years old). This Act effected unprecedented repatriation of human remains from the British Museum to Australia and New Zealand. Secondly, the opening of the *National Museum of the American Indian* (NMAI) the same year signaled a shift in authority and expertise in metropolitan museums. The role of the curator as *connoisseur* was substituted with the involvement of Native voices in contemporary readings of artifacts. As part of this shift in curatorial practice, the British Museum initiated a series of meetings with "source communities" under various headings to enrich, diversify, and strengthen the knowledge base for their collections from the Pacific Northwest Coast, under headings such as *Arctic Clothing* and *Powwows,* etc. In an unpublished report, the Curator at that time explains:

> To one of these, Andrea Sanborn, who ran U'mista, came. We said, "Will you come and talk about what you've been doing?" And so she came and she saw the mask, and we talked about the mask, and we got to know each other, and then she went back and then she asked for a loan of the mask. And all of this happened in the context of the 2004 Human Tissue Act, and so there was already a sort of institutional change. It was a catalyst. There was no connection at all between making a long term loan of the mask and

the Human Tissue Act, but it acted as an offstage catalyst. (Jonathan King, unpublished report on file with the authors)

Rather than a challenge, or even a threat, to the collection management at the British Museum, this loan request was turned into an opportunity for the museum, *transforming* a claim underwritten by a technology of sovereignty into a technology of reformation. In the words of the curator at that time: "If you invest the time and energy and effort into bringing the originators of the collections back together with the collections, everybody benefits enormously, there's no question about that. The objects come to mean much more to the museum, and to the originating community and above all to the general public" (Jonathan King, unpublished report on file with the authors).

The new curatorial practice was to organize objects and people in such a way that new knowledge is yielded by either bringing members from First Nations on the Pacific Northwest Coast to London and/or lending them materials in exchange for information, if they have their own museums with compatible standards. This technology of reformation entails not only enlisting and involving First Nations in the collections-based knowledge production about "their own cultural heritage," but also communicating this knowledge to metropolitan audiences as in the recent exhibition *Where the Thunderbird Lives*. Essentially, it is about creating a common regime of engagement (Thévenot, 2015) in which both the holding institution and the "source community" have investments. With reference to the transformation mask, the curator explains: "when William Wasden, Jr. saw it, he was able to describe how it was made, how it was used, and who might have made it, so immediately, the mask became much more interesting than it had ever been before in the British Museum." The holding museum also made the loan conditional on certain conditions being met by the receiving museum. The curator explains:

> U'mista is an accredited museum, it actually has most of the masks and returned regalia on open display. And we said, "No, we don't want the mask to be on open display, it must be in a case," and so a case was built for it. There was that one simple issue, but before it was placed on display, it was received in the Big House in the traditional manner and then put on display. (Thévenot, 2015)

Here we see how the holding institution, through the enrollment of the claimant in knowledge production for public consumption and a series of material conditions, which have to be consented to for the loan to take place, transforms a claim into a technology of reformation. We recall once again, in this context, Carl Schmitt's characterization of sovereignty as the exception to rules

(Schmitt, 2005 [1922]). It is clear that the transformation mask has been transformed, moved from the sign of cultural property as a means for producing sovereign subjects to the sign of cultural heritage. The formal ownership issue and the term repatriation has been substituted with a common regime of engagement. Nevertheless, this transformation leaves open Andrea Sanborn's question in Athens: "How can world histories make sense if they remain in pieces, spread about the world with their fragmented stories? Let us all tell our own stories."

5 Trajectories

"We are not naive. The day may come when this world will create other visions, other concepts of what is proper, of what comprises a cultural patrimony and of human creativity."

Melina Mercouri (1982)

At first glance, the three case histories unfolded in the previous section – that of the return of medieval manuscripts to Iceland, the UTIMUT transfer of museum artifacts to Greenland, and the transformation of the Kwakwaka'wakw transformation mask – may appear to corroborate the prediction by Prott and O'Keefe in 1992, that cultural heritage would supersede cultural property; a prediction later affirmed as fact by other legal scholars.

We propose to complicate such linear, teleological narratives by moving from a legal to an historical definition of cultural property and cultural heritage. From an historical perspective, we submit that cultural property and cultural heritage:

i. are distinct, if overlapping, formations within an overarching patrimonial field

ii. that developed under distinct historical conditions (the one in the aftermath of WWII, the other in the aftermath of decolonization),

iii. producing separate regimes (the one proceeding from the Hague Convention, the other from the World Heritage Convention)

iv. and distinct forms of expertise (the one primarily legal, the other primarily curatorial),

v. which belong to different rationalities of government (the one liberal, the other neoliberal)

vi. and take a very different approach to the formation of patrimonial and political subjects (the one producing sovereign subjects in the mold of the liberal modern state, with rights, territories, borders, and property, the other producing subjects entangled in dense networks of neoliberal/postcolonial forms of governance).

vii. The one employs return, restitution, and repatriation as a technology of
    sovereignty, the other employs capacity building, education, collaboration,
    reciprocity, exchange, and the infusion of expertise as a technology of
    reformation.

As is evident from Section 4, individual case trajectories can and do move
between the sign of cultural property and the sign of cultural heritage. It would
be a mistake, however, to jump to the conclusion that this movement is
unilinear: from property to heritage. The empirical evidence shows that social
actors draw on both concepts, both formations, pulling or pushing objects back
and forth between the signs of cultural heritage and cultural property and
subjects between reformation and sovereignty.

The Medieval Manuscripts: More Return, More Cooperation

The return of the medieval manuscripts from Denmark to Iceland is a case in
point. At the time of writing, the government of Iceland has renewed its claim
for the return of the Icelandic manuscripts that remained in Denmark after the
partition of the manuscript collection. In a government meeting on August 28,
2019, the Minister of Culture received approval to seek negotiations with the
government of Denmark for the "recovery" of more manuscripts from the
Arnamagnean Institute in Copenhagen.

Renewed interest in the return of the medieval manuscripts was, in part at
least, sparked by the temporary loan in 2018 of two major "gems" from the
Arnamagnean manuscript collection in Denmark: a manuscript of the Prose
Edda of Snorri Sturluson (a principal source for medieval mythology and
poetics) and a manuscript of Njál's Saga (the most renowned of the medieval
sagas). They were greeted at the airport in Iceland by the armed special forces
of the police and escorted to Iceland's National Gallery, where they were
centerpieces in a special exhibition for the centennial anniversary of Iceland's
sovereignty in 1918, entitled "Blossoming. Iceland's 100 Years as a Sovereign
State."

When the two manuscripts arrived on loan from Denmark in 2018, the
director of the Árni Magnússon Institute in Reykjavík, Guðrún Nordal, spoke
to journalists about how much they moved her, how emotional it made her to
have them in her hands. When a reporter asked her whether she wasn't tempted
not to return them, she responded: "Yes, that is very tempting. I admit it, I have
to be honest. But they are only here for a visit. We only borrowed them"
(Pétursson, 2018; our translation).

Ironically, the loan – a textbook example of cooperation, reciprocity, exchange,
and entanglement – seems to have helped to move the trajectory of the manuscript

Figure 27 "Yes, that is very tempting. I admit it, I have to be honest. But they are only here for a visit. We only borrowed them." Director of the Árni Magnússon Institute in Reykjavík, Guðrún Nordal, celebrates the homecoming of two gems from the Arnamagnean manuscript collection in Copenhagen for a temporary exhibition in 2018 for the centennial anniversary of Iceland's sovereignty. Photograph by Jóhanna Ólafsdóttir. Courtesy of the Árni Magnússon Institute for Icelandic Studies.

case back under the sign of cultural property. When Iceland's Minister of Culture was reminded, in an interview on Icelandic state radio in August 2019, that the partition agreement between Denmark and Iceland stipulated that the settlement was final, and specifically required that Icelanders would not claim any further return, the Minister answered: "It was a very bitter dispute and a very difficult political dispute. There were very many Danes who wanted us to have all the manuscripts back home. The Danish nation was split over this. Not everyone agreed with the solution" (Hagalín Björnsdóttir, 2019; our translation). The Minister noted, moreover, that "one of the things that has been happening in the museum field internationally is that national treasures like these are increasingly being returned to their countries of origin" (Valgerðardóttir, 2019; our translation).

Some three weeks later, on September 17, 2019, the Ministers of Culture from Iceland and Denmark sat down for a meeting in Copenhagen; Guðrún Nordal, the director of the Árni Magnússon Institute also took part. "Opinion has shifted in the nearly fifty years that have passed since the first manuscripts were returned to Iceland – both in Denmark and in Iceland," the Icelandic

Figure 28 Iceland's Minister of Culture, Lilja Alfreðsdóttir, poses with Guðrún Nordal, Director of the Árni Magnússon Institute in Reykjavík, and a vellum manuscript in August 2019 in a photo opportunity arranged before launching a new claim for the return of Icelandic medieval manuscripts remaining in Denmark. Photograph by Sigurður Stefán Jónsson. Courtesy of the Árni Magnússon Institute for Icelandic Studies.

Minister claimed after the meeting, expressing optimism that "we will be able to recover more manuscripts" (Sævarsson, 2019; our translation; see also Hilmarsdóttir, 2019).

From shared cultural heritage, equitably partitioned and jointly curated, the Icelandic Minister of Culture has manifestly moved the medieval manuscripts back under the sign of cultural property – to be reclaimed and "recovered". Previously, the manuscripts were framed through a technology of reformation as objects of collaboration, capacity building, and exchange of expertise, tying the subjects of heritage more closely together. Now, with the renewal of the claim for their "recovery" and "return home," they are deployed once more in a technology of sovereignty.

Needless to say, this is not the final word on the manuscripts. In Iceland itself, some philologists and historians object. Thus, Már Jónsson, professor of history at the University of Iceland, says it is "an awful idea and absurd to depart from the consensus surrounding the agreement" from 1961; instead, he warns, "the emphasis ought to be on more cooperation, not on dispute. This turn of phrase, to return home, places the entire case back on square one, for this is the same claim that Icelandic authorities made in the 1940s and 1950s" (Ritstjórn Eyjunnar, 2019; our translation).

The outcome of the ministerial meeting in Copenhagen in September 2019 demonstrates, however, the "curatorial cunning" of the Danish approach, for it seems once again to slide the case under the sign of cultural heritage – promising "more cooperation." According to a press release from Iceland's Ministry of Education and Culture, the ministers agreed to set up a "joint commission on the common cultural heritage" of the two nations, which will be charged with "reviewing and strengthening their cooperation in the heritage field," proposing "future arrangements for the conservation of the manuscripts that are now in Denmark," considering how the nations can cooperate in the cultivation of their languages in the face of globalization and "how to use the common cultural heritage of Iceland and Denmark to that end" (Iceland's Ministry of Education and Culture, Press Release, 2019; our translation).

"Loan Me the Sculptures": Revisiting the Acropolis

We contend that the trajectory of the manuscripts case over the course of the last century demonstrates the analytical usefulness of the distinction we have drawn between cultural property, on the one hand, and cultural heritage, on the other. Another example may reinforce our contention. It takes us back to the Parthenon sculptures, which, like the manuscripts, returned to international politics and the media spotlight in 2019.

We left these sculptures in Section 2 at the *Athens International Conference on the Return of Cultural Objects to their Countries of Origin* in March 2008. Greece invited to this conference key actors to take forward the debate and timed it to coincide with the opening of the new Acropolis Museum where, as we noted, a nation-state asserted its sovereign right through elaborate staging and extravagant expenditure. The terminology had shifted, with Minister Michalis Liapis making the claim not merely on behalf of the Greek people but "in the name of the world's cultural heritage; a universal demand and a global debt to Greece."

The following year, Greece was hit hard by sovereign debt crisis. It was not until after the end of a decade-long bailout regime, complete with austerity and surrender of fiscal sovereignty, that a Greek government raised the issue of the Parthenon sculptures once more. The motivation, this time, is the government's preparations for the bicentennial celebration marking Greece's independence in 1821; another performance of a nation-state's sovereignty, comparable to the centennial celebration of sovereignty in Iceland that played a part in reopening the manuscripts case.

In an attempt to break the impasse, the leader of Greece's newly formed right-wing government, Prime Minister Kyriakos Mitsotakis, took a critical step toward moving the sculptures, in our terms, from the sign of cultural property to the sign of cultural heritage. Instead of demanding their return or restitution, he announced his intention to request them on loan. To make the proposition more palatable, he suggested a quid-pro-quo: "In this context, given the significance of 2021, I will propose to Boris [Johnson, the UK's Prime Minister]: 'As a first move, loan me the sculptures for a certain period of time and I will send you very important artefacts that have never left Greece to be exhibited in the British Museum'" (Smith, 2019).

This move is reminiscent of the case trajectory of the Kwakwaka'wakw claim for the return of the transformation mask, originally couched in terms of cultural property as a technology of sovereignty (see Section 2) but subsequently shifting under the sign of cultural heritage as the British Museum successfully countered the claim with an offer of a renewable loan; an offer of exchange and engagement, extending museological networks of expertise and management (see Section 4). The Greek Prime Minister's offer of reciprocity (with "very important artefacts that have never left Greece") may perhaps also be read as an offer of collateral for the sculptures, a guarantee for their eventual return. The rationale he gives, however, is quite different: "Our wish and ambition is to create the necessary conditions for Greek cultural heritage to travel the world and in so doing convey the great and essential contribution of our country to western civilisation." Referring to circulation and exchange, he adopts the cultural heritage discourse of the British Museum to ask for the Parthenon sculptures on their terms: "The Acropolis doesn't necessarily solely belong to Greece," he adds. "It's a monument of global cultural heritage. But if you really want to see the monument in its unity you have to see what we call the Parthenon sculptures in situ . . . it's a question of uniting the monument" (Smith, 2019).

The leader of the opposition, former prime minister Alexis Tsipras, immediately condemned the move as a "naïve initiative" that "allows the British Museum to appear as the rightful owner." Indeed, a British Museum spokesperson confirmed to *The Telegraph* that "a pre-condition for any loan is the acceptance of the lending institution's ownership," adding: "No museum or gallery in the world would loan objects unless the other institution that was borrowing them accepted ownership" (Squires, 2019).

Prime Minister Mitsotakis' casual reference to his British counterpart, Boris Johnson, may relate to speculation in Greece a few weeks earlier, when these men both took office, that as a committed philhellene, Johnson might take more kindly than his predecessors to the Greek claim (Chrysopoulos, 2019). Indeed, when Johnson moved into the Prime Minister's office in London's Downing Street he reportedly took with him a 23.5 kilo plaster-cast bust of Pericles of Athens. At the time of writing, Johnson has not publicly commented on Mitsotakis' request to "loan me the sculptures." As it happens, however, a younger Boris Johnson helped to put up for debate the question of where these sculptures belong. Quite literally so, for as the newly elected president of the Oxford University Union, a student-led debating society, he organized a debate in 1986 on the return of the Parthenon sculptures, inviting none other than Melina Mercouri to address the audience – Greece's Culture Minister and the most impassioned and eloquent proponent for Greece's sovereign claim for the return of cultural property.

"You must understand what the Parthenon Marbles mean to us," she told the members of the debating society. "They are our pride. They are our sacrifices. They are our noblest symbol of excellence. They are a tribute to the democratic philosophy. They are our aspirations and our name. They are the essence of Greekness." Following the conventions of classical rhetoric, Mercouri struck down one by one the arguments against return, noting at one point that:

Figure 29 Melina Mercouri, Greece's Culture Minister speaks with the President of the Oxford Union Society, a young Boris Johnson, before she addressed the Union at the University of Oxford, Britain, June 12, 1986. Photograph by REUTERS/Brian Smith.

Of late, a new theory has been proposed, this one is a beauty. Mr Gavin Stamp (I shall have the honour of meeting him tonight) proposes the notion that modern Greeks are not descendants of Pericles.

Wow! Our marbles have been taken. Who will lay claim to the bones of our ancestors? As Minister of Culture, I hereby invite Mr Stamp to come to Athens. I will arrange prime time on television for him to tell . . . the Greek people who they are." (Mercouri, 1986)

Contagion and Homeopathy: Unity, Integrity, Wholeness

The transfer of the manuscripts from Denmark to Iceland and the non-transfer of the Parthenon sculptures from the British Museum to Greece illustrate how particular case trajectories may shift back and forth between rights-based claims and resolutions under the sign of cultural property, on the one hand, and ethical claims and solutions under the sign of cultural heritage, on the other; between the exclusive and the shared; between sovereignty (a form of agency without expectation of reciprocity) and reformation (with cooperation, capacity building, exchange, reciprocity, and entanglement). Far from portraying such shifts in terms either of linear progress or as an implosion of any meaningful distinction, we argue that there is significant analytical purchase to be gained from an historically grounded and theoretically informed understanding of the distinction between the two terms.

Cultural heritage and cultural property represent, we have argued, two distinguishable (if entangled) patrimonialities. If the history of the one (cultural property) is longer than the history of the other (cultural heritage), that does not entail that the latter has replaced, is replacing, or will replace the former. Rather, we contend, social actors (states, tribes, museums, populations, scholars, experts, professionals, politicians) draw strategically on both, sometimes in a call-and-response relation, sometimes both at once.

Rereading the various case trajectories, we are struck by the extent to which the discourses of cultural heritage and cultural property both deploy a rhetoric of integrity. Integrity, unity, and wholeness are values shared equally by proponents of repatriation and apologists for the universal museum. Under the sign of cultural property, the "homecoming" of cultural objects is envisioned as a reunification in which that which has been "scattered" will be made "whole again". In contrast, under the sign of cultural heritage, the integrity of the collection will be "violated" if the museum is "ravaged" through transfer of individual objects to source communities (while further relationships may be forged through loans, exchanges, and infusion of expertise). To give another example, a commission of the Danish Ministry of Education created to respond to Iceland's demand for the return of the manuscripts published an opinion in

1951 where it warned that many Danes would experience even a partial return "as an intervention breaking up a large whole built up through the centuries, of which the Icelandic manuscripts make up only one part" (Commission of the Danish Ministry of Education, 1951, p. 94; our translation).

As regards the value of integrity in cultural property claims, recall the appeal by Andrea Sanborn, speaking on behalf of the Kwakwaka'wakw First Nation at a conference in Athens: "The very soul of our culture remains fragmented until all the pieces can be reunited, repatriated, and returned home. . . . and our lives become whole again." There is no mistaking the intimate relation here between the objects and the subjects. Once returned and reunited, the transformation mask and other cultural property will make the Kwakwaka'wakw nation whole again. In much the same way, mutilated and dispersed under Ottoman rule, the return of the Parthenon marbles "to the blue sky of Attica," in the words of Melina Mercouri, "where they will be a structural and functional part of a unique whole" is indivisible from the unity and sovereignty of the Greek people. The return of the medieval manuscripts from the former colonial capital is referred to in Iceland as a "homecoming" and intimately linked to the political sovereignty of the Icelandic nation. Meanwhile, as leader of the Scottish National Party, Alex Salmond pledged to "continue campaigning for a united set of Lewis Chessmen in an independent Scotland." And the leader of the Native Hawaiian organization Hui Malama maintained that when all the objects and ancestral bones sitting in federal repositories and in museums around the world would be back in Native Hawaiian soil, "we will have our *kulāiwi* (homeland) back."

The agency of objects is palpable in these declarations. Under the sign of cultural property, objects are agentive. They act on the subjects of cultural property – the nation or tribe – and vice versa. This is because they are indivisibly connected, even when they are separated; in claiming the object and calling for its return, the subject declares its sovereignty. In reuniting the object, the subject is made whole. The relationship may be characterized as metonymical; the object and the subject are intimately associated and their association is based on contiguity. Thus, for example, the Parthenon marbles do not "represent" the people of Greece, no more than the transformation mask "represents" the Kwakwaka'wakw First Nation or the Lewis Chessmen represent the Scots; torn out of the Parthenon in Athens, the marbles "are the essence of Greekness," and the spirits of ancestors can only rest when the ceremonial masks and regalia are returned to the Kwakwaka'wakw. The relationship, in other words, is not metaphorical. In Sanborn's words, "the very soul of our culture remains fragmented until all the pieces can be reunited, repatriated and returned home."

This is, moreover, why the argument of objects as "ambassadors," representing the ethos of a culture in far-away places and acting as a magnet for tourism to those places, has never had much traction in the return and restitution debates, except in the eyes of the keepers. The same goes for "digital repatriation"; offers of digital surrogates or representations do not acknowledge the metonymical nature of the relationship of the object to the subject under the sign of cultural property.

There is another distinction on which we might draw in this context, parallel to that between metonymical and metaphorical relations. We have in mind James G. Frazer's distinction in *The Golden Bough* (1922) between what he characterized as two branches of sympathetic magic: contagious and homeopathic. In Frazer's words, the physical basis of contagious magic is "a material medium of some sort which . . . is assumed to unite distant objects and to convey impressions from one to the other" (Frazer, 1922, p. 38). Contagious magic, Frazer contends, "proceeds upon the notion that things which have once been conjoined must remain ever afterwards, even when quite dissevered from each other, in such a sympathetic relation that whatever is done to the one must similarly affect the other" (p. 39).

The analogy to the dynamics of cultural property is noteworthy. The object–subject relation under the sign of cultural property operates on principles quite similar to those which Frazer described as contagious magic. If, as Benedict Anderson portrayed them, nations are imagined communities (Anderson, 1991 [1983]), then cultural property gives such communities physical substance through an act of displacement. We might say that objects of cultural property metonymize their subjects in such a way that they may be seen, touched, and experienced as real. If returned, the homecoming of the objects will therefore restore the unity and integrity of the subjects – make them whole. "The most familiar example of contagious magic," Frazer offers by way of illustration, "is the magical sympathy which is supposed to exist between a man and any severed portion of his person, as his hair or nails; so that whoever gets possession of human hair or nails may work his will, at any distance, upon the person from whom they were cut" (Frazer, 1922, p. 38). By this logic, it also stands to reason that demanding the return of cultural property is a technology of sovereignty: to claim cultural property is to reclaim control of one's future and of oneself.

Conversely, the "magic of the museum" may, in Frazer's terms, be characterized as homeopathic. The work of the museum, and the work of heritage more broadly, is the work of representation through condensation and combination. The relationship of museum collections to subjects and their histories is in this sense metaphorical, rather than metonymical. Following Barbara Kirshenblatt-Gimblett (as we have done in Section 3), to recycle "sites, buildings, objects, technologies, or ways of life" as heritage is to give these things a new lease on life, not as what they once were, but as "representations of themselves" (Kirshenblatt-Gimblett, 1998, p. 151). As a metacultural practice, cultural heritage points beyond itself to a culture it claims to represent or a history it can recount. Moreover, a hallmark of heritage is "the problematic relationship of its objects to the instruments of their display" (p. 156).

In this context, we could refer back to the relationship of Vimbuza healing to the festival used to represent it as intangible heritage and to UNESCO's intangible heritage list that combines it with various other practices and expressions to represent the diversity of human creative powers. Or we may refer to the relationship of the British Museum to the Parthenon sculptures, to the Lewis Chessmen, and to the Kwakwaka'wakw transformation mask. In the collection of the British Museum, these objects may be arranged – through the metaphorical operations of condensation and combination – to represent human civilization and endeavor in a universal account of history. Their second life as representation rests on the loss of their former function and their combination through the instrument of display – the exhibit, the catalogue, the website – in "a collection with a worldwide civic purpose." In the words of Neil MacGregor, the museum's former director, this purpose is: "to allow visitors to address through the filter of history, both ancient and more recent, key questions of contemporary politics and international relations, to assess and consider their place in the world and to see the different parts of that world as indissolubly linked" (MacGregor, 2004, p. 7). If, in national museums, objects created in particular times and local contexts are combined and deployed metaphorically to narrate the history of a national subject, the "universal museum" metaphorizes the objects to represent multiple subjects, ultimately synthesized in the universal subject of humanity.

We may refer back to Frazer's theory of sympathetic magic: the principle of homeopathic (as opposed to contagious) magic, according to Frazer, "is that like produces like, or, in other words, that an effect resembles its cause." We suggest that the metaphorical operations of condensation and combination capture the ways in which objects refer to subjects under the sign of cultural heritage. Another way to think of this work of representation is as homeopathic magic. To work its magic, the museum must guard its wholeness; picked apart, it loses some of its magical powers.

To sum up, if the rhetoric of integrity unites the discourses of cultural heritage and cultural property, that integrity is differently located. For the former, the integrity of the collection must be maintained for the museum to fulfill its civic role. For the latter, with its evocative language of original wholes and scattered parts, by reuniting the object with its original context and function the repatriated artifact makes the subject whole again.

References

Agamben, Giorgio (1998). *Homo Sacer: Sovereign Power and Bare Life.* Stanford: Stanford University Press.

Agrawal, Arun (2005). "Environmentality: Community, Intimate Government, and the Making of Environmental Subjects in Kumaon, India." *Current Anthropology*, **46**(2), 161–190.

Agrawal, Arun, and Clark C. Gibson (2001). "The Role of Community in Natural Resource Conservation." In Arun Agrawal and Clark C. Gibson, eds., *Communities and the Environment: Ethnicity, Gender, and the State in Community-Based Conservation.* New Brunswick, NJ: Rutgers University Press, pp. 1–31.

Anderson, Benedict (1991 [1983]). *Imagined Communities: Reflections on the Origin and Spread of Nationalism.* New York: Verso.

Arendt, Hannah (1958). *The Human Condition.* Chicago: University of Chicago Press.

Arnold, Matthew (1998 [1869]). "Culture and Anarchy." In John Storey, ed., *Cultural Theory & Popular Culture. A Reader*, 2nd ed. Athens: University of Georgia Press, pp. 6–11.

Baron, Robert, and Nicholas Spitzer (2007). *Public Folklore.* Jackson: University Press of Mississippi.

Beardslee, Thomas (2014). Questioning Safeguarding: Heritage and Capabilities at the Jemaa El Fnaa, Ph.D. diss. The Ohio State University.

Beardslee, Thomas (2016). "Whom Does Heritage Empower, and Whom Does It Silence? Intangible Cultural Heritage at the Jemaa el Fnaa, Marrakech." *International Journal of Heritage Studies*, **22**(2), 89–101.

Bendix, Regina (2000). "Heredity, Hybridity, and Heritage from One Fin-de-Siècle to the Next." In Pertti J. Anttonen, ed., *Folklore, Heritage Politics, and Ethnic Diversity.* Botkyrka: Multicultural Centre, pp. 37–54.

Bennett, Tony (2003). "Culture and Governmentality." In Jack Z. Bratich, Jeremy Packer, and Cameron McCarthy, eds., *Foucault, Cultural Studies, and Governmentality.* Albany: State University of New York Press, pp. 47–63.

Beretninger og Kundgørelser vedrørende Styrelsen af Grønland 1913–1917. Copenhagen: J.H. Schultz.

Bessmann, Sandra, and Mathias Rota (2008). "Espace public de la medina. La place 'Jemaa el Fna.'" In Blaise Dupuis and Sophie Marchand, eds., *Etude de terrain. La Gentrification dans la Median de Marrakech.* Neuchâtel: Université de Neuchâtel, Institut de géographie, pp. 113–126.

Bhabha, Homi K. (1994). *The Location of Culture*. London: Routledge.

Biolsi, Thomas (2004). "Political and Legal Status ('Lower 48' States)." In Thomas Biolsi, ed., *A Companion to the Anthropology of American Indians*. New York: Blackwell, pp. 231–247.

Blake, Janet (2000). "On Defining the Cultural Heritage." *International and Comparative Law Quarterly*, **49**(1), 61–85.

Blake, Janet (2015). *International Cultural Heritage Law*. Oxford: Oxford University Press.

Botchway, Karl (2001). "Paradox of Empowerment: Reflections on a Case Study from Northern Ghana." *World Development*, **29**(1), 135–153.

British Museum Press Release (2018). Accessed March 10, 2020. web .archive.org/web/20190623184440/www.britishmuseum.org/about_us/ news_and_press/statements/the_lewis_chessmen.aspx

Brown, Michael (2003). *Who Owns Native Culture?* Cambridge, MA: Harvard University Press.

Bulkeley, Harriet, and Arthur P. Mol (2003). "Participation and Environmental Governance: Consensus, Ambivalence and Debate." *Environmental Values*, **12**(2), 143–154.

Caldwell, David H, Mark A Hall, and Caroline M. Wilkinson (2009). "The Lewis Hoard of Gaming Pieces: A Re-examination of their Context, Meanings, Discovery and Manufacture." *Medieval Archaeology*, **53**(1): 155–203.

Callon, Michel, Andrew Barry, and Don Slater (2002). "Technology, Politics and the Market: An Interview with Michel Callon." *Economy and Society*, **31** (2): 285–306.

Choplin, Marie-Astrid, and Vincent Gatin (2010). "L'espace public comme vitrine de la ville marocaine: Conceptions et appropriations des places Jemaa El Fna à Marrakech, Boujloud à Fès et Al Mouahidine à Ouarzazate." *Norois. Environnement, aménagement, société*, 214(1), 23–40. http://norois.revues.org/3095

Chrysopoulos, Philip (2019). "The UK's New PM Loves Greece – But Will He Return the Marbles?" *Greek Reporter*, July 23, 2019. Accessed March 4, 2020. https://eu.greekreporter.com/2019/07/23/the-uks-new-pm-loves- greece-but-will-he-return-the-marbles-video/

Comaroff, John L., and Jean Comaroff (2009). *Ethnicity, INC*. Chicago: University of Chicago Press.

Commission of the Danish Ministry of Education (1951). *Betænkning vedrørende de i Danmark beroende islandske håndskrifter og museumgenstande*. Afgivet af den af undervisningsministeriet under 13. Marts 1947 nedsatte kommission. Copenhagen: J.H. Schultz A/S Universitets-Bogtrykkeri.

Coombe, Rosemary J. (2003). "Works in Progress: Traditional Knowledge, Biological Diversity, and Intellectual Property in a Neoliberal Era." In Richard Warren Perry and Bill Maurer, eds., *Globalization under Construction: Governmentality, Law and Identity*. Minneapolis: University of Minnesota Press, pp. 273–314.

Coombe, Rosemary J. (2009). "The Expanding Purview of Cultural Properties and Their Politics." *Annual Review of Law and Social Science*, **5**, 393–412.

Coombe, Rosemary J., and Lindsay M. Weiss (2015). "Neoliberalism, Heritage Regimes, and Cultural Rights." In Lynn Meskell, ed., *Global Heritage: A Reader*. Hoboken, NJ: Wiley-Blackwell, pp. 43–69.

Cornwall, Andrea (2008). "Unpacking 'Participation': Models, Meanings and Practices." *Community Development Journal*, **43**(3), 269–283.

Cornwall, Andrea, and Deborah Eade (2010). *Deconstructing Development Discourse: Buzzwords and Fuzzwords*. Oxford: Oxfam GB.

Cortés-Vázquez, Jose, Guadalupe Jiménez-Esquinas, and Cristina Sánchez-Carretero (2017). "Heritage and Participatory Governance: An Analysis of Political Strategies and Social Fractures in Spain." *Anthropology Today*, **33**(1), 15–18.

Cranmer Webster, Gloria (1992). "From Colonization to Repatriation." In Gerald McMaster and Lee-Ann Martin, eds., *Indigena: Contemporary Native Perspectives*. Vancouver: Douglas and McIntyre, pp. 25–37.

Davíðsdóttir, Sigrún (1999). *Håndskriftsagens saga i politisk belysning*. Odense: Odense Universitetsforlag.

Declaration on the Importance and Value of Universal Museums (2004). ICOM News, no. 1, p. 4. Accessed March 4, 2020. http://archives.icom.museum /pdf/E_news2004/p4_2004–1.pdf

De Carlo, Giancarlo (1980). "An Architecture of Participation." *Perspecta*, **17**, 74–79.

Derrida, Jacques (1978). *Writing and Difference*. Chicago: University of Chicago Press.

Eriksen, Anne (2014). *From Antiquities to Heritage: Transformations of Cultural Memory*. New York: Berghahn Books.

Foster, Michael Dylan (2015). "Imagined UNESCOs: Interpreting Intangible Cultural Heritage on a Japanese Island." *Journal of Folklore Research*, **52**(2), 217–232.

Foucault, Michel (1991 [1978]). "Governmentality." In Graham Burchell, Colin Gordon, and Peter Miller, eds., *The Foucault Effect: Studies in Governmentality*. London: Harvester Wheatsheaf, pp. 87–104.

Frazer, James G. (1922). *The Golden Bough: A Study in Magic and Religion*. 3rd ed., abridged. New York: The Macmillan Company.

Friedmann, John (2011). *Insurgencies: Essays in Planning Theory*. Abingdon-on-Thames: Routledge.

Frigo, Manlio (2004). "Cultural Property v. Cultural Heritage: A "Battle of Concepts" in International Law?" *Revue Internationale de la Croix-Rouge /International Review of the Red Cross*, **86**(854), 367–378.

Gabriel, Mille (2008). "Introduction: From Conflict to Partnership." In Mille Gabriel and Jens Dahl, eds., *UTIMUT: Past Heritage – Future Partnerships. Discussions on Repatriation in the 21st Century*. Copenhagen: International Work Group for Indigenous Affairs and Greenland National Museum & Archives.

Geismar, Haidy (2013). *Treasured Posessions: Indigenous Interventions into Cultural and Intellectual Property*. Durham: Duke University Press.

Geismar, Haidy (2015). "Anthropology and Heritage Regimes." *Annual Review of Anthropology* **44**, 71–85.

Gilman, Lisa (2015). "Demonic or Cultural Treasure? Local Perspectives on Vimbuza, Intangible Cultural Heritage, and UNESCO in Malawi." *Journal of Folklore Research*, **52**(2), 199–216.

GoFundMe (2015). "Hui Malama I Na Kupuna O Hawaii Nei." Deactivated. Accessed March 12, 2020. www.gofundme.com/f/ue7tg9s

Goytisolo, Juan (2002). "Entrevista de Arcadi Espada a Juan Goytisolo." *La Espia del Sur*. Accessed October 15, 2017. web.archive.org/web/20021020065811/www.geocities.com/laespia/goytisolo2.htm

Greenfield, Jeanette (2013 [1989]). *The Return of Cultural Treasures*, 3rd ed. Cambridge: Cambridge University.

Hafstein, Valdimar (2012). "Cultural Heritage." In Regina Bendix and Galit Hasan-Rokem, eds., *A Companion to Folklore*. Malden, MA: Blackwell Publishing, pp. 500–519.

Hafstein, Valdimar (2014). "Protection as Dispossession: Government in the Vernacular." In Deborah Kapchan, ed., *Cultural Heritage in Transit. Intangible Rights as Human Rights*. Philadelphia: University of Pennsylvania Press, pp. 25–57.

Hafstein, Valdimar (2018). *Making Intangible Heritage: El Condor Pasa and Other Stories from UNESCO*. Bloomington: Indiana University Press.

Hagalín Björnsdóttir, Sigríður (2019). "Handritin heim – aftur?," 30 August 2019. Accessed March 4, 2020. www.ruv.is/frett/handritin-heim-aftur

Hálfdánarson, Guðmundur (2003). "Handritamálið – endalok íslenskrar sjálfstæðisbaráttu." *Gripla*, **14**, 175–196.

Hálfdanarson, Guðmundur (2015). "Þjóðnýting menningararfsins. Norræn miðaldamenning og sköpun nútímaþjóðernis." In Ólafur Rastrick and Valdimar Tr. Hafstein, eds., *Menningararfur á Íslandi. Gagnrýni og greining*. Reykjavík: University of Iceland Press, pp. 39–70.

Hall, Mark (2010). "A Passion for Chess Pieces." National Museums Scotland Blog. Accessed March 10, 2020. https://blog.nms.ac.uk/2010/08/05/a-pas sion-for-chess-pieces/

Handler, Richard (1988). *Nationalism and the Politics of Culture in Quebec*. Madison: University of Wisconsin Press.

Healey, Patsy (1997). *Collaborative Planning: Shaping Places in Fragmented Societies*. Hampshire: Palgrave Macmillan.

Hertz, Ellen (2015). "Bottoms, Genuine and Spurious." In Nicolas Adell, Regina F. Bendix, Chiara Bortolotto, and Markus Tauschek, eds., *Between Imagined Communities and Communities of Practice. Participation, Territory and the Making of Heritage*. Göttingen: Universitätsverlag Göttingen, pp. 25–58.

Hilmarsdóttir, Sunna Kristín (2019). "Lilja fundaði með danska menntamálaráðherranum um framtíð handritanna," *Vísir*, 17 September 2019. Accessed March 4, 2020. www.visir.is/g/2019190918934/lilja-fundadi-med-danska-mennta-mala-rad-herranum-um-fram-tid-hand-ritanna

Hinton, Rachel (1995). "Trades in Different Worlds: Listening to Refugee Voices." *PLA NOTES*, pp. 21–26.

Hitchens, Christopher (1987). *The Elgin Marbles: Should They be Returned to Greece?* London: Chatto & Windus.

Hodge, Margaret (2008). "Lewis Chessmen are pawns in Salmond's political game." *The Scotsman. Scotland on Sunday*, 27 January. Archived on Elginism website. Accessed March 12, 2020. www.elginism.com/similar-cases/are-the-lewis-chessmen-becoming-political-pawns/20080128/945/

Holtorf, Cornelius (2012). "The Heritage of Heritage." *Heritage & Society*, **5** (2), 153–174.

Iceland's Ministry of Education and Culture (2019). Press Release: "Fundað um framtíð handritanna," 17 September 2019. Accessed March 4, 2020. www .stjornarradid.is/efst-a-baugi/frettir/stok-frett/2019/09/17/Fundad-um-fram tid-handritanna/

Jacknis, Ira (2000). "Repatriation as Social Drama: The Kwakiutl Indians of British Columbia, 1922–1980." In Devon A. Mihesuah, ed., *Repatriation Reader: Who Owns American Indian Remains?*. Lincoln: University of Nebraska Press, pp. 266–281.

Jacknis, Ira (2002). *The Storage Box of Tradition. Kwakiutl Art, Anthropologists, and Museums, 1881–1981.* Smithsonian Series in Ethnographic Inquiry. Washington, DC: Smithsonian Institution Scholarly Press.

Jackson, Robert (2018). "Retain or Return: It's complicated," *The Art Newspaper,* May (no 301). Accessed March 11, 2020. www.theartnewspaper.com/com ment/retain-or-return-it-s-complicated

Jiménez-Esquinas, Guadalupe (2019). "Límites y limitaciones de la participación ciudadana o cuando la arqueología comunitaria molesta: el caso de Costa dos Castros." In Cristina Sánchez-Carretero, et al., eds., *El imperativo de la participación en la gestión patrimonial.* Santiago de Compostela: Editorial CSIC, pp. 109–142.

Jolly, Margaret (2017). "Moving Objects: Reflections on Oceanic Collections." In Elisabetta Gnecchi-Ruscone and Anna Paini, eds., *Tides of Innovation in Oceania. Value, Materiality, and Place.* Acton: Australian National University Press, pp. 77–114.

Johnson, Greg (2007). *Sacred Claims: Repatriation and Living Tradition.* Charlottesville and London: University of Virginia Press.

Jones, Peter Blundell, Doina Petrescu, and Jeremy Till (2005). *Architecture and Participation.* Abingdon-on-Thames: Routledge.

Kapchan, Deborah (2014). "Intangible Heritage in Transit: Goytisolo's Rescue and Moroccan Cultural Rights." In Deborah Kapchan, ed., *Cultural Heritage in Transit. Intangible Rights as Human Rights.* Philadelphia: University of Pennsylvania Press, pp. 177–194.

Kirshenblatt-Gimblett, Barbara (1998). *Destination Culture: Tourism, Museums, and Heritage.* Berkeley: University of California Press.

Kirshenblatt-Gimblett, Barbara (2006). "World Heritage and Cultural Economics." In Ivan Karp and Corinne Kratz, eds., *Museum Frictions: Public Cultures/Global Transformations.* Durham: Duke University Press, pp. 161–202.

Kjær, Birgitte (2002). "'Håndskriftsagen' set fra Danmark." *Nordisk Museologi* **2**, 8–16.

Klein, Barbro (2006). "Cultural Heritage, the Swedish Folklife Sphere, and the Others." *Cultural Analysis* **5**, 57–80.

Li, Tania Murray (2001). "Boundary Work. Community, Market, and State Reconsidered." In Arun Agrawal and Clark C. Gibson, eds., *Communities and the Environment. Ethnicity, Gender, and the State in Community-Based Conservation.* New Brunswick, NJ: Rutgers University Press, pp. 157–179.

Lowenthal, David (1998). *The Heritage Crusade and the Spoils of History.* Cambridge: Cambridge University Press.

Lowthorp, Leah (2015). "Voices on the Ground: Kutiyattam, UNESCO, and the Heritage of Humanity." *Journal of Folklore Research*, **52**(2), 157–180.

MacGregor, Neil (2004). "The British Museum," *ICOM News*, **1**, 7. Accessed March 4, 2020. http://archives.icom.museum/pdf/E_news2004/p7_2004-1 .pdf

McDermott, Melanie Hughes (2001). "Invoking Community. Indigenous People and Ancestral Domain in Palawan, the Philippines." In Arun Agrawal and Clark C. Gibson, eds., *Communities and the Environment. Ethnicity, Gender, and the State in Community-Based Conservation*. New Brunswick, NJ: Rutgers University Press, pp. 32–62.

Mercouri, Melina (1982). "Address of Mme. Melina Mercouri, Minister of Culture and Sciences of Greece, to the World Conference on Cultural Policies, organized by UNESCO in Mexico, July 29, 1982, on the submission by Greece of a Draft Recommendation on the Return of Cultural Property to its Country of Origin." Melina Mercouri Foundation. Accessed March 11, 2020. http://melinamercourifoundation.com/en/speeches1/

Mercouri, Melina (1984). "Greece's Claim to the Elgin Marbles. Q&A: Melina Mercouri," *New York Times*, March 4, Section 4, 9. Accessed March 12, 2020. www.nytimes.com/1984/03/04/weekinreview/q-a-melina-mercourt-greece-s-claim-to-the-elgin-marbles.html

Mercouri, Melina (1986). "Melina's Speech to the Oxford Union." The Parthenon Marbles. Accessed March 4, 2020. www.parthenon.newmentor.net/speech .htm

Merriman, Nick (2004). *Public Archaeology*. Abingdon-on-Thames: Routledge.

Michener, Victoria J. (1998). "The Participatory Approach: Contradiction and Co-Option in Burkina Faso." *World Development*, **26**(12), 2105–2118.

Miller, Daniel, ed. (1995). *Worlds Apart: Modernity through the Prism of the Local*. London: Routledge.

Mitchell, Timothy (1998). "Fixing the Economy." *Cultural Studies*, **12**(1), 82–101.

Morgan, Lynn M. (2001). "Community Participation in Health: Perpetual Allure, Persistent Challenge." *Health Policy and Planning*, **16**(3), 221–230.

Morgunblaðið (1971, 20 March). "Fögnum við handritunum eða stendur okkur á sama?," 10–11.

Morgunblaðið (1971, 21 April). "Ég og Jörgen Jörgenssen ákváðum í bíl á leið frá Þingvöllum að málið yrði að leysa," 10.

Morgunblaðið (1971, 21 April). Special issue: "Handritablað."

Morgunblaðið (1971, 22 April). "Vær saa god, Flatöbogen," 1/18.

Morgunblaðið (1971, 22 April). "Sá orðstír, sem Ísland gat sér á miðöldum, mun aldrei deyja," 12.

National Museum of Denmark. Etnografisk samlings beretningsarkiv. Unpublished archival sources.

Nebelong, Henrik (2002). "'Haandskriftssagerne' i bagklogskabens lys." In Peter Garde, Mogens Koktvedgaard, and Oluf Engell, eds., *Mindevaerdige Retssager*. Copenhagen: Forlaget Thomson, Gad Jura, pp. 127–142.

Ólason, Vésteinn. (2002). "Håndskriftenes Hjemkomst: Vitenskapelig og Ideologisk Belysning." *Nordisk Museologi*, **2**, 3–7.

Palonen, Ville (2013). "Winds of Change over Morocco." *Blue Wings Gift Issue*, December 2013. Published online September 30, 2016: https://issuu .com/finnair_bluewings/docs/blue_wings_10_2013_pieni/19

"Periodic reporting on the Convention for the Safeguarding of the Intangible Cultural Heritage: Madagascar" (2012). Report submitted on 15/12/2012 and examined by the Committee in 2013. *UNESCO: Intangible Cultural Heritage*. Accessed May 29, 2017. https://ich.unesco.org/en/state/madagas car-MG?info=periodic-reporting#pr–2013–2013

"Periodic reporting on the Convention for the Safeguarding of the Intangible Cultural Heritage: Vietnam" (2013). Report submitted on 15/12/2013 and examined by the Committee in 2014. *UNESCO: Intangible Cultural Heritage*. Accessed May 29, 2017. https://ich.unesco.org/en/state/viet-nam-VN?info=periodic-reporting#pr–2012–2012

Pentz, Peter, ed. (2004). *Utimut – Return: The Return of More Than 35.000 Cultural Objects to Greenland*. Gylling: The National Museum of Denmark, Greenland National Museum and Archives and UNESCO.

Pétursson, Heimir Már (2018). "Freistandi að skila Dönum ekki lánuðum handritum aftur," *Vísir* 5 July 2018. Accessed March 4, 2020. www.visir.is /g/2018180709378

Povinelli, Elizabeth (2002) *The Cunning of Recognition: Indigenous Alterities and the Making of Australian Multiculturalism*. Durham: Duke University Press.

Prott, Lyndel V., ed. (2009). *Witnesses to History: A Compendium of Documents and Writings on the Return of Cultural Objects*. Paris: UNESCO.

Prott, Lyndel V., and Patrick J. O'Keefe (1992). "'Cultural Heritage' or 'Cultural Property'?" *International journal of cultural property*, **1**(2), 307–320.

Richardson, Lorna Jane, and Jaime Almansa-Sánchez (2015). "Do You Even Know What Public Archaeology Is? Trends, Theory, Practice, Ethics." *World Archaeology*, **47**(2), 194–211.

Risler, Julia, and Ares, Pablo (2013). *Manual de mapeo colectivo: recursos cartográficos críticos para procesos territoriales de creación colaborativa*. Buenos Aires: Tinta Limón.

Ritstjórn Eyjunnar (2019). "Sagnfræðiprófessor segir hugmynd Lilju afleita," *DV* 3 September 2019. Accessed March 4, 2020. www.dv.is/eyjan/2019/09/ 03/sagnfraediprofessor-segir-hugmynd-lilju-afleita-aukid-hilluplass-kallar-ekki-fleiri-handrit/

Robertson, Alastair (1996). "Now Scotland Asks for its Chess Set Back," *Sunday Times*, 1 December.

Rose, Nikolas (1996). "Governing 'Advanced' Liberal Democracies." In A. Barry, T. Osbourne, and N. Rose, eds., *Foucault and Political Reason: Liberalism, Neo-Liberalism and Rationalities of Government*. Chicago: University of Chicago Press, pp. 37–64.

Rose, Nikolas (1999). *Powers of Freedom: Reframing Political Thought*. Cambridge: Cambridge University Press.

Rosing, Emil, and Peter Pentz (2004). "The Museum Collaboration of Denmark and Greenland." In Peter Pentz, ed., *Utimut – Return: The Return of More Than 35.000 Cultural Objects to Greenland*. Gylling: The National Museum of Denmark and the Greenland National Museum and Archives and UNESCO, pp. 23–30.

Sævarsson, Sigurður Bogi (2019). "Vongóð eftir samtöl við menntamálaráðherrann," Morgunblaðið 30 August 2019. Accessed March 4, 2020. www.mbl.is/frettir/innlent/2019/08/30/vongod_eftir_samtol _vid_menntamalaradherrann/

Salmond, Alex (2007). "Sabhal Mor Ostaig Lecture 2007. Given by The First Minister, Alex Salmond MP, MSP." Sabhal Mor Ostaig. Accessed March 10, 2020. www.smo.uhi.ac.uk/smo/naidheachd/fiosan/smo-lecture2007_b.html

Sánchez-Carretero, Cristina, José Muñoz-Albaladejo, Ana Ruiz-Blanch, and Joan Roura-Expósito, eds. (2019). *El imperativo de la participación en la gestión patrimonial*. Santiago de Compostela: Editorial CSIC.

Sarr, Felwine, and Bénédicte Savoy (2018). *The Restitution of African Cultural Heritage: Toward a New Relational Ethics*. Paris: Ministère de la culture. Accessed March 11, 2020. http://restitutionreport2018.com/sarr_savoy_en .pdf

Schmitt, Carl (2005 [1922]). *Political Theology: Four Chapters on the Concept of Sovereignty*. Chicago: University of Chicago Press.

Schmitt, Thomas (2005). "Jemaa el Fna Square in Marrakech: Changes to a Social Space and to a UNESCO Masterpiece of the Oral and Intangible Heritage of Humanity as a Result of Global influences." *The Arab World Geographer* **8**(4), 173–195.

Scottish Parliamentary Business Report (2008). Meeting of the Parliament, Thursday 18 September 2008. Session 3. Accessed March 10, 2020. www .parlamaid-alba.org/parliamentarybusiness/report.aspx?r=4814&mode=pdf

Select Committee on Culture, Media and Sport (2000). "Memorandum submitted by Glasgow City Council." UK Parliament, House of Commons. Accessed March 12, 2020. https://publications.parliament.uk/pa/cm199900/cmselect/cmcumeds/371/0051808.htm

Sigurðsson, Gísli, and Vésteinn Ólason, eds. (2004). *The Manuscripts of Iceland*. Reykjavik: Arni Magnusson Institute in Iceland.

Simon, Nina (2010). *The Participatory Museum*. Santa Cruz: Museum 2.0.

Smith, Helena (2019). "Greece offers sculpture swap in bid for Parthenon marbles," *The Observer* 1 September 2019. Accessed March 4, 2020. www.theguardian.com/culture/2019/aug/31/greece-sculpture-swap-athens-partheon-elgin-marbles-boris-johnson

Smith, Laurajane (2006). *Uses of Heritage*. London: Routledge.

Soko, Boston (2014). *Vimbuza: The Healing Dance of Northern Malawi*. Lilongwe: Mzuni Press.

Squires, Nick (2019). "Greece Would Have to Acknowledge British Museum Ownership if It Wants a Loan of the Elgin Marbles," *The Telegraph* 3 September 2019. Accessed March 4, 2020. www.telegraph.co.uk/news/2019/09/03/greece-has-acknowledge-british-museum-ownership-wants-loan-elgin/

St. Clair, William (1998). *Lord Elgin and the Marbles*. Oxford: Oxford University Press.

Tebbaa, Ouidad (2010). "Le patrimoine de la place Jemaa El Fna de Marrakech: Entre le matériel et l'immatériel." *Quaderns de la Mediterrània*, **13**, 51–58.

Thévenot, Laurent (2015). "Making Commonality in the Plural, on the Basis of Binding Eengagements." In Paul Dumouchel and Reiko Gotoh, eds., *Social Bonds as Freedom: Revising the Dichotomy of the Universal and the Particular*. New York: Berghahn, pp. 82–108.

TripAdvisor User Review (2013). "Aminated." April 9, 2013. www.tripadvisor.co.uk/ShowUserReviews-g293734-d318047-r157242126-Jemaa_el_Fnaa-Marrakech_Marrakech_Tensift_El_Haouz_Region.html#

UK Parliament Early Day Motions (2010). "Lewis Chessmen," EDM #892, tabled 22 February 2010. House of Commons. 2009–2010 Session. Accessed March 12, 2020. www.parliament.uk/edm/2009–10/892

UK Parliament Westminster Hall (2010). "Repatriation of Historical Objects," Westminster Hall, House of Commons. 10 March 2010, vol. 507.

U'mista Cultural Society. n.d. "The Meaning of 'U'mista'." Accessed March 12, 2020. http://archive.umista.ca/

UNESCO (2001). *Proclamation of Masterpieces of the Oral and Intangible Heritage of Humanity. Guide for the Presentation of Candidature Files*. Paris: Intangible Heritage Section, Division of Cultural Heritage, UNESCO.

UNESCO (2002a). *Guidelines for the Establishment of Living Human Treasures Systems*. Paris: UNESCO Section of Intangible Cultural Heritage and Korean National Commission for UNESCO.

UNESCO (2002b). "Intangible Cultural Heritage: Priority Domains for an International Convention. Impacts of the First Proclamation on the Nineteen Masterpieces Proclaimed Oral and Intangible Heritage of Humanity." Expert Meeting, Rio de Janeiro, 2002. Document RIO/ITH/2002/INF.

UNESCO (2008). UNESCOPRESS Press Release No. 112.

UNESCO Intangible Cultural Heritage (2008). "Vimbuza Healing Dance." Accessed March 10, 2020. https://ich.unesco.org/en/RL/vimbuza-healing-dance–00158

Valgerðardóttir, Sunna (2019). "Lilja ræddi við danska ráðherrann um handritin," Fréttastofa RÚV, 29 August 2019. Accessed March 4, 2020. www.ruv.is/frett/lilja-raeddi-vid-danska-radherrann-um-handritin

Webb, Timothy (2002). "Appropriating the Stones: The "Elgin Marbles" and the English National Taste." In Elazar Barkan and Ronald Bush, eds., *Claiming the Stones – Naming the Bones*. Los Angeles: Getty Research Institute, pp.51–96.

Winter, Tim (2015). "Heritage Diplomacy." *International Journal of Heritage Studies*, **21**(10), 997–1015.

Acknowledgements

We did not know it at the time, but this work began in 2002 when we first met at a summer school in Lammi, Finland, and discovered that we were pursuing similar themes within our doctoral programs in Folklore at Berkeley and Cultural Anthropology at Columbia, respectively. Our discussions matured in 2005/6, when we swapped insights and experiences from our common engagement with the UN body *World Intellectual Property Organization* (WIPO, Geneva) over tea in lower Manhattan. However, it took several years of fermentation and a number of visits to the public thermal pools in Reykjavík in the summers of 2018 and 2019 before the manuscript took its final shape. In the course of almost two decades working on this book (as it turns out), we have accumulated more debts than we could mention here. However, we wish to express our indebtedness to the many individuals and institutions who directly or indirectly contributed to the content, who have helped us, encouraged us and inspired us along our way, and in particular:

- In Hawai'i, individuals working for the former Native Hawaiian repatriation organization *Hui Mālama*: the Po'o Alealoha and Noe Noe. Former and current staff at the Office of Hawaiian Affairs: Apolei Bargamento and Kai Markell. Former and current staff at the Bishop Museum: Betty Lou Kam, Mara Mulrooney and William Y. Brown. Former and present staff at the 'Iolani Palace: Stuart Chang. For the application of NAGPRA to Hawai'i, Toni Palermo and Sara Collins assisted.
- In Providence, Museum Director Tracey Keough, Keeper Marilyn Massaro, Assistant Joanne Wilcox, former Superintendent of Parks Nancy Derrig, former Mayor Buddy Cianci, Prof. Martha Joukowski and Prof. Carolyn Fluhr-Lobban for consultations in their respective areas of expertise.
- In Reykjavik, Rósa Þorsteinsdóttir, Sigurður Stefán Jónsson, Gísli Sigurðsson, Vésteinn Ólason and Jónas Kristjánsson at the Árni Magnússon Institute for Icelandic Studies; and colleagues in the department of folkloristics/ethnology and museum studies: Guðrún Whitehead, Kristinn Schram, Ólafur Rastrick, Sigurjón B. Hafsteinsson, Terry Gunnell, as well as Jón Þór Pétursson and in particular Áki Karlsson for helping us pull together the manuscript.
- In Copenhagen, former and current staff at the National Museum of Denmark: Torben Lundbæk, Poul Mørk, Bente Wolff, Rolf Gilberg, Inger Wulff, Bodil Valentiner, Jesper Kurt Nielsen and former Director Per Kristian

Madsen. For introductions to UTIMUT, in particular Jørgen Meldgaard, Einar Lund Jensen, Eigil Knuth and Peter Pentz.

- In Nuuk, former and current staff at the Greenland National Museum & Archives: Jens Heinrich, Claus Andreasen, Deputy Christian Koch Madsen and Director Daniel Thorleifsen.
- In Athens, former and current staff at the Archaeological Service of the Greek Ministry of Culture in particular Elena Korka. For introduction to the legal aspects of the Parthenon case, in particular George Bisos.
- For assistance with understanding the letter and the spirit of NAGPRA we want to acknowledge: former and current Members of the NAGPRA Review Committee: Armand Minthorn, Martin Sullivan, Rosita Worl and Attorneys at the Solicitor's Office Carla Mattix and Tobias Halvarson.
- For assistance with understanding the work of UNESCO, we want to thank the following: Rieks Smeets, Guðný Helgadóttir, Einar Hreinsson, Alissandra Cummins, Guido Carducci and Jens Boel.
- For assistance with understanding museums and the issues of return/restitution from the perspective of the International Committee of Museums (ICOM) we acknowledge former and current members: Per Rekdal, Daniel Papuga, Leif Parelli, Geoffrey Lewis, Harrie Leyden, Beatrice Murphy and Richard "Rick" West Jr.
- For giving us the occasion to think about the property/heritage divide/relation in the first place, we want to thank Jane Andersen and Haidy Geismar. For helping us think through some of the arguments presented here, we thank Regina Bendix and Galit Hasan-Rokem. For extending an invitation to contribute to the series, we are very grateful to Kristian Kristiansen, Michael Rowlands and Ola Wetterberg.
- For encouragement and inspiration at various points when needed, each in their different ways: Alan Dundes, Barbara Kirshenblatt-Gimblett, Barbro Klein, Bosse Lagerqvist, Brinkley Messick, Claire Smith, Deborah Kapchan, Dorothy Lippert, Dorothy Noyes, Elizabeth Povinelli, Elliott Oring, Enid Schildkrout, Fabio Mugnaini, Fiona Macmillan, Francisco Vaz da Silva, Fred Myers, Helle Porsdam, Ida Nicolaisen, Ingrid Martins-Holmberg, James Clifford, John Lindow, Kay Turner, Kirsten Hastrup, Laurajane Smith, Lila Abu-Lughod, Lynn Meskell, Mahmood Mamdani, Mick Taussig, Nadia Abu El-Haj, Nan Rothschild, Nélia Susana Dias, Ólafur Rastrick, Paul Turnbull, Pertti Anttonen, Peter Jan Margry, Regina Bendix, Robert Baron, Rodney Harrisson, Rosemary Coombe, Susan Wright, Terence D'Altroy, Terry Gunnell, Tim Lloyd, and Tok Thompson.

- For their generosity and insightful comments: the three anonymous reviewers for the Cambridge Element Series. The book would no doubt be better if we had been able to follow all their suggestions.
- For allowing us to use their fieldwork photographs, we are grateful to: Jonathan King, Lisa Gilman and Leah Lowthorp, as well as various photographers who have made their work available with Creative Commons licenses.
- For letting us get away with this, we are grateful as always to the Copenhagen Business School and the University of Iceland. We would also like to recognize that the Wenner-Gren Foundation for Anthropological Research supported fieldwork in Rhode Island and Hawaii as well as the write-up of that research.
- For their support, their patience, their love, and for putting up with the other guy's presence for many consecutive breakfasts and dinners in Amager and Miðstræti (or, in turn, their own guy's absence), we thank our families: Lene, Malthe, Malou, Brynhildur, Hannes, and Ragnheiður.

Cambridge Elements ☰

Critical Heritage Studies

Kristian Kristiansen
University of Gothenburg

Michael Rowlands
UCL

Francis Nyamnjoh
University of Cape Town

Astrid Swenson
Bath University

Shu-Li Wang
Academia Sinica

Ola Wetterberg
University of Gothenburg

About the Series

This series focuses on the recently established field of Critical Heritage Studies. Interdisciplinary in character, it brings together contributions from experts working in range of fields, including cultural management, anthropology, archaeology, politics, and law. The series will include volumes that demonstrate the impact of contemporary theoretical discourses on heritage found throughout the world, raising awareness of the acute relevance of critically analysing and understanding the way heritage is used today to form new futures.

Cambridge Elements ᛤ

Critical Heritage Studies

Printed in the United States
By Bookmasters